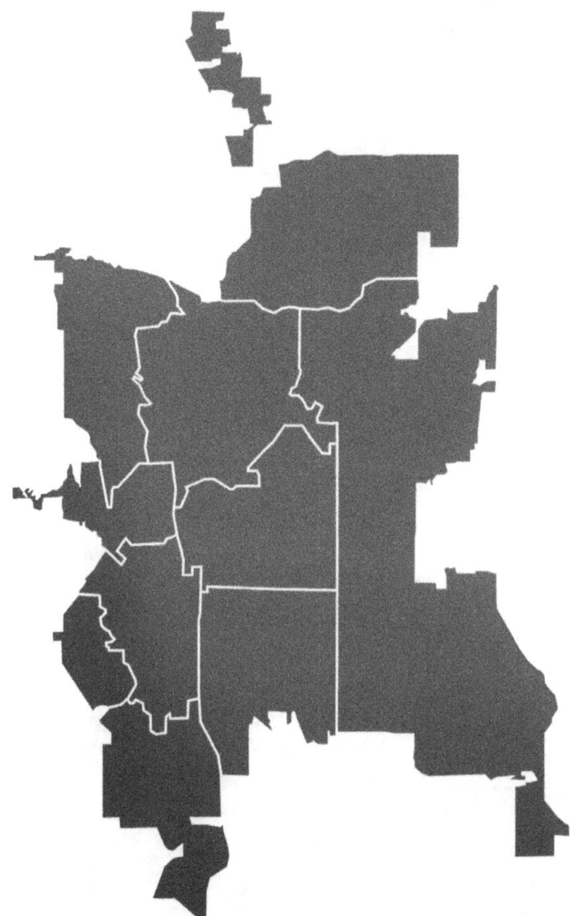

REAL ESTATE
IN COLORADO SPRINGS

Your extensive, professional guide
to purchasing a home in 2021

DARREN BRYCE, REALTOR®
BROKER ASSOCIATE

By wisdom a house is built, and through understanding it is established; through knowledge its rooms are filled with rare and beautiful treasures.

–PROVERBS 24:3–4

Copyright © 2021 Darren Bryce

For permissions, contact:
darren@brokerdarren.com, 719-659-4000

Visit the author's website: www.brokerdarren.com

Sellstate Alliance Realty & Property Management
1155 Kelly Johnson Blvd #206, Colorado Springs, CO 80920

Book Format & Cover Design: Melody Christian, Finicky Fox Design, finickyfoxdesign.com
ISBN: 9798594074149

TABLE OF CONTENTS

INTRODUCTION

IT WAS 1993 as my wife and I sat patiently in Bill's office at Norwest Mortgage, awaiting information about a refinance we were contemplating. Bill turned to us in frustration and told us he was having difficulty with a spreadsheet that showed us the costs of doing the loan. I told him I would take a quick look at it, and upon my evaluation, I found a simple mistake in the calculation area and corrected it quickly. He looked at me and said, "do you want a job?"

That was the beginning of an adventure in mortgage lending and then real estate sales that has occupied my life for the past 25 years.

I worked with Bill for a year learning about mortgages, construction financing, how to work with builders, and how to close loans in a timely fashion. I was then approached by the manager of a competing mortgage company, and she made me an offer to run a small satellite branch of MICAL Mortgage in Tehachapi, California—my home. This was quite the adventurous journey as I serviced the Mojave Dessert and Tehachapi (pronounced just how it's spelled), originating mortgages for approximately five years. I helped complete two master certificates of reasonable value (master appraisals for VA financing), for two housing developments in California City, working with Norwest Financial and MICAL Mortgage—huge tasks for a new loan officer. I loved servicing the public and helping Realtors® become a success. This career path seemed to suit me well.

Then one day I showed up to my office where I was met by a moving van and my manager. She looked down as she proceeded in telling me that the entire company had been sold, and they were closing our offices.

Well, what now?

I had the office leased for another month. As I thought through my time as a mortgage lender, I realized just how much I loved to watch Realtors® working with buyers and sellers, helping them realize their real estate dreams. I am creative and love marketing great services to the public. What would be the best move for me now?

Real estate.

Yes! The idea excited me. Shortly thereafter I opened Innovative Real Estate with another very capable Realtor® and broker, and off I went on my new adventure.

Another year passed and the brutal reality of running my own business set in. I was looking for the next opportunity.

One morning, I got the usual gossip report from my title representative that a broker I used to do loans for, Al, lost his entire group of agents. I decided to give him a call to see if he would meet with me. As I was discussing the idea of us joining forces with him over lunch, I became quite annoyed by his persistent fussing with his keys. Finally, I asked him, "Al, what are you doing?" He told me he was trying to get me a key to his office so I could get right to it. (How's that for joining forces?)

With excitement, I joined Cardinal Realtors and worked to build a strong business over the next few years. I loved serving my friends and neighbors, meeting their real estate needs in Tehachapi, California! It brought me so much joy.

Then my wife and I decided we wanted to investigate moving to a community with more options for colleges and fun for our family. Colorado Springs, Colorado, here we come.

This was a very difficult move for a man who had lived his entire life no further than an hour from where he was born. But God called us to move, so off we went. I met a great employing broker in Colorado Springs and began my adventure in real estate in the "Springs" in 2004. After several years with Morning Star Real Estate, I looked for a better opportunity with a company with a forward-looking business model. That's when I found Sellstate Alliance Realty in 2010, and I have been with this outstanding company ever since. I am on the Board of Advisors and have most often been a part of the 1% club of top producing agents, which has in return allowed me to be blessed to receive many awards—evidence of the many families I get to help each year.

WHY I WROTE THIS BOOK

I desire to help home buyers and sellers by providing them with information and details about the most complicated transaction they will ever be involved in—*the real estate transaction*. In the following pages, I will be covering a lot of ground about many different types of transactions. Although there will be tons of information, **this is not a book that is all inclusive.** The information is deemed reliable, but not *all* details apply to *all* transactions. I hope to share my experience in a way that educates and helps lead you in the right direction to a successful real estate closing.

If any of this that you are about to delve into feels overwhelming, that's okay. My job as your *Expert Advisor*™ is to pay attention to all these details for you, and to make sure they are all handled with professionalism and expertise. You can relax and know that I have your best interests at heart.

In fact, my real estate business is all about protecting your dreams and making them a reality. Real estate is unique in that it helps you realize a dream that you have built around yours and your family's lifestyle. My goal is to ensure that you understand every step of the process so that at closing, you know that you have bought the right house, at the right price, in the right condition—reaching that dream for your family.

HOW TO READ THIS BOOK

I don't want this book to seem as though it was written as a sales brochure (it's not). But there *is* a difference in how agents work and the value that they provide. So I utilize my experience and unique services to help educate you throughout the book.

Not all Realtors® offer the same services, and you should consider this when hiring one. We are all independent business owners under the direction of our employing brokers, led by real estate law and the code of ethics we adopt to as Realtors®. Please also understand that not all real estate agents are Realtors® and it is important that you choose one that is. Visit the National Association of Realtors® to learn more about the professionalism set up for its members here: www.nar.realtor/about-nar Each state has its own organization that participants belong to. The State of Colorado's website is here: www.coloradorealtors.com

The book is organized very simply into chapters that highlight types of property with facts and figures that apply based on the publication date of this book. I have a very real passion for real estate, and want to make sure that your questions are answered. Please don't hesitate to reach out to me with questions, and make sure to visit my website for additional free resources and more mentioned throughout this book.

Take notes, learn a lot, and get excited about the process that lies ahead of you! I'm here to help as your personal, professional Realtor®.

Being in the real estate business for over 25 years, I've got quite the stories to tell! I'll probably share a few when we meet in person, but for now, look out for some of my favorite (and craziest stories) throughout the book.

MY FIRST SALE

DOUBLE-SIDED WITH MY BUSINESS, INNOVATIVE REAL ESTATE

Deciding to go into real estate was a big move for me. I had seen the frustration experienced by agents in my community as I originated loans for them. When the company I had been working for shut down, I had to make a choice about my future. Real estate sales seemed interesting and challenging, so I made the decision to go into the real estate sales business.

I always have been blessed with a creative mind. Opening Innovative Real Estate gave me the opportunity to be creative in business. One part of the model I created was a program designed to work with for-sale-by-owner customers. Providing flyers, signs, websites, and marking ideas to these clients gave me the opportunity to develop relationships that would hopefully lead to full-service contracts.

My very first deal in real estate was an example of this program coming to fruition. My first week in business was exciting, to say the least, and it greatly exceeded my expectations. I met my first FSBO client and provided him lots of great information. I developed a relationship with this client, and he agreed to work with me if I brought him a ready and willing buyer.

The next day I received a referral from a friend at church. After meeting with these buyers, I immediately realized that the FSBO I had just met owned the perfect property for them. Off we went to look at the home.

It was perfect.

Within two weeks of opening our doors, I had secured a double-sided real estate sale transaction from my innovative marketing plan to for-sale-by-owner customers. Boy was that a rush. Off I headed into my new passion for real estate, knowing that this was my calling and I was right where I was meant to be.

REAL ESTATE OVERVIEW

REAL ESTATE **CAN BE DEFINED AS LAND,** as well as any improvement affixed to the land. This can include houses, buildings, landscaping, etc. I have seen many types of real estate in my career and am fascinated with it all. We enjoy the rights of being able to purchase and sell real estate in the United States of America, and this right sets us apart from many countries in the world. Selling real estate is a career that is exciting and challenging and has been my life for many years, and prayerfully, will be for many more to come. As a Realtor®, we are guided in how we perform our duties through law, instruction, and by the National Association of Realtors® Code of Ethics.

NAR's (National Association of Realtors®) code of ethics was adopted in 1913 and sets the standards that members use when operating with each other and the public. The document begins by stating:

Under all is the land. Upon its wise utilization and widely allocated ownership depend the survival and growth of free institutions and of our civilization. REALTORS® should recognize that the interests of the nation and its citizens require the highest and best use of the land and the widest distribution of land ownership. They require the creation of adequate housing, the building of functioning cities, the development of productive industries and farms, and the preservation of a healthful environment.

This document was drafted many years ago and has been adapted several times, but its intent is very clear. It states that "…In the interpretation of this obligation, REALTORS® can take no safer guide than that which has been handed down through the centuries, embodied in the Golden Rule, 'Whatsoever ye would that others should do to you, do ye even so to them'."

I take this obligation with a high level of seriousness and believe it sets the tone for our profession and how we conduct business. You don't find this type of commitment in many other industries.

As a Realtor®, we are required to study the Code of Ethics and are tested on our knowledge of it every four years. I don't believe the public is aware of this requirement, but it sets us apart as professionals that have a true interest in doing "the right thing." Above and beyond, this is our individual approach to our business in how we conduct ourselves professionally, with each other, and the public.

So often, the public has a very poor view of Realtors®. In some cases, this reputation is well deserved. But unfortunately, it gets applied to us all. I hope that you take the time to discuss with your Realtor® how they perform their duties and how they handle the entire process of working with sellers and buyers of real estate—from the beginning of the process to closing the transaction, and even afterwards. There is a difference between Realtors®. I hope to provide you with my vision about how I service you during and after the most important transaction of your life: buying and selling real estate.

I am part of a national organization of professional real estate advisors called the NAEA. Part of this program includes looking at all the areas that a home buyer must consider when purchasing or building a home. This program is called the Expert Advisor Smart Home Buying Strategy™. You can look at this strategy later in the book under the section, "Working with Darren Bryce as Your 'Buyer's Agent'" where I lay out in detail what makes me different than other Realtors® in our area.

WHAT KIND OF HOME IS THIS?

NEVER HAVE I *ALMOST* SOLD A HOME LIKE THIS ONE.

I received a lead and called to discuss listing a home in Yoder. I ran the comps to get an idea of the value range, then went to look at the home. The home was... nice. Very strange split floorplan with an unusual loft, but genuinely *nice*.

I sold it in quick order. The inspector showed up and began the inspection. The first thing he noticed was the foundation. There actually wasn't one. Yes, you read that right. *The house didn't have a foundation.*

A few 4x4's and sheeting, and *that* was considered the foundation. One of the neighbors came over about the time of this revelation, and approached me to tell me an interesting story.

Apparently this home was a mobile home with FIVE additions, and was set on a wood pallet (granted, an exceptionally large wood pallet). I stood there confused... what now? I wasn't yet familiar with properties in Colorado and had to learn this lesson the hard way.

The deal fell apart (naturally). Fully disclosed up front, the property would need to be a cash only transaction. Lesson learned... check the foundation, and make sure it isn't an oversized wood palette?

But at least the house was nice...

CHAPTER 1:
A Look at the Purchasing Process

PURCHASING REAL ESTATE, of any kind, can be a very difficult and intimidating process to review. It's all about taking one step at a time. Thoroughly read these sections, and utilize my website for detailed worksheets that you can use when you visit homes or lots in our area.

BUDGET

First, you need to be advised on budgeting how much it is going to cost you to maintain and take care of your home. Items such as utility costs, association dues, appliance repairs and replacements, painting the outside of your home, water heater and central heating cleaning and repair, deck refinishing, and landscape maintenance are just some of the costs to consider. These costs can be evaluated by looking at:

- the current condition and age of the home
- the home's amenities
- HOA costs
- the climate of the area
- the building materials used in the construction of the home

Even a vacant lot has costs associated with it including weed mitigation, drainage control, and making sure it isn't being used by someone to dump their waste. Once you meet with your lender, you will know what the estimated payment will be for the price range you are considering. Always be real about your budget and overestimate expenses.

INVESTMENT PERSPECTIVE

It is important to look at the investment perspective of buying your home. A full market analysis of the home you are looking at buying will be provided to you by me. With it, we will consider ways that you can accelerate your home equity build and do home improvements that will net you a return later. Selecting the proper loan program can be key for the future when it is time to sell. Avoiding pre-payment penalties, adjustable mortgages, and interest-only loans will keep your equity-build position strong.

> **After closing, I will keep you updated as to the current market value of your home. Call me anytime for a comparative market analysis: 719-659-4000.**

SELECTING THE RIGHT HOME AT THE RIGHT PRICE

There are so many issues to look at when buying a home. Some questions to ask as you review the home:

- How close is the home to retail shopping, amenities, and primary employers in the area?
- What is the neighborhood crime rate like? (View crime reports for neighborhoods at myneighborhoodupdate.net)
- What upgrades and features of the home are favorable, and will help sell the home in the future? Is the floorplan favorable?
- What "feeling" does the home give you as you tour it?
- What condition is the home in?
- Is the home manufactured? Does that effect how the property retains its value?
- Is the home the most expensive in the area?
- What price can we negotiate, and what terms are going to be acceptable for the seller to get your offer accepted?

> With my experience working with many buyers and sellers, I know what most buyers are looking for in a home, and what gives a home that "wow" factor for them. I perform a "mini" inspection as we walk through the home so that you don't enter a transaction that will fall apart later, and at least have a heads up about the variables we'll face in the process. A full analysis of the entire property from location to the small details of quality construction can protect your investment for years to come.

OFFER STRATEGIES

The implications of the details in the contract we present to a seller are extremely important, and something you need to be able to understand. Items like seller concessions, home warranties, timing issues, and understandability of the contract can get your offer accepted. The type of property you are purchasing makes a difference with your strategy. If the property is a bank-owned property, I advise clients to lessen the conditions, sometimes even waiving inspections, if the price is right. You must be able to look at the type of seller and their position to be able to submit a successful offer. Pre-approvals with a local lender are critical to a seller in this current marketplace. Making sure you use a reputable lender with a great reputation locally to make your offer more appealing to the seller is often vital (and something I will help you with as an expert negotiator).

BUYERS PURCHASE WARRANTY

So, you're buying your dream home, right? What if it's not quite what you thought it was, even though we walked through all the precautionary steps above? That's thankfully okay with my comprehensive buyer warranty. I will sell your home for minimal fees and save you thousands of dollars. I will help you locate a new home and even pay for your home warranty (for appliances, etc.). This warranty will help you have some peace of mind about your purchase. View warranty details at: www.brokerdarren.com/buyerwarranty. *Note: you will still have to pay a selling broker commission and some fees from the real estate company, but I do my best to keep this at a bare minimum for you.*

CLOSING YOUR TRANSACTION

There are so many pieces to the puzzle. Working with an agent that has a system to keep track of all those pieces is critical for a successful closing. Ask ahead of time what system is in place to ensure this successful closing.

- Are all the contract conditions met?
- Has a walk-through been scheduled to make sure the property hasn't changed? Yes, sellers and movers do have accidents, and you need to know about it before closing so that a resolution can be made for the issues.
- Have utilities been transferred?
- When has the closing been scheduled with the title company, and does it work for your schedule?
- What expectations about closing all need to be set?
- Do you need to take funds in for closing? How much and what type of funds?

What do you, the buyer, expect when sitting at the table with the seller? In Colorado, we are a table-closing state, meaning that when you leave the table at closing, the property is yours and most everything is completed. The title company still must record the deed and send the funds and documents to all parties that need them. You also agree to go back and sign something if there is a mistake, but otherwise it is a done deal.

AFTER CLOSING SERVICES

You will get the recorded title and a copy of the title insurance package after closing. Keep this for future reference. Usually your interest is tax deductible, so your taxes will look more favorable before you owned a home.

If you purchased a home warranty, you will want to keep a copy handy in case of a problem. There are specific procedures for filing a claim with a warranty company that you will need to know, and I can help you with that process.

You can request a predictive analysis evaluation for the value of your house later, after you have owned it for a while.

> I provide a free market and predictive analysis yearly to my clients so that they can keep track of the appreciation they are realizing. Make just one extra payment per year and you would be surprised of the net effect in the loan balance. Your lender and I will stay in contact with you so that you can check these items as often as you like.

Ready to move again? I discount my commission on your sale when you buy another home from me.

Are you just wondering what is going on in the current market? Great, I have an app that you can use to stay up-to-date on market activity in your neighborhood or a neighborhood you are considering moving to.

PLEASE STAY IN TOUCH

I truly enjoy the relationships established during the transaction with my clients, and like to share experiences on a platform like Facebook with you (facebook.com/brokerdarren). And remember, I value your referrals to friends and family.

MY INFAMOUS CLIENT

THAT ONE TIME I SOLD A LOG HOME TO A FAMOUS SAX PLAYER

Living just a couple of hours away from L.A., our little town was accustomed to famous performers seeking a nice mountain home away from the city. Tom had an amazing talent for playing the saxaphone and for producing big events. I was pleased to meet him in my office to discuss building a log home on a mountainside in the Tehachapi, California mountains. He was amazing, nice, and knew just what he wanted. I referred him to my favorite builder and off the project started.

Log homes are awfully expensive to build and the cost per square foot will not compare to other homes. We ran into a problem. The project would not appraise for anywhere near the cost. He really wanted this home for recording and inspiration and went ahead with the home anyway. He ended up with a beautiful, log home with tremendous views. Sometimes it is worth paying more for a home that really is an inspiration for you even though the value won't compare to other homes in the area.

CHAPTER 2:
Loan Programs

DISCUSSING REAL ESTATE would be near impossible without looking into the options available for financing your new home. Even if you aren't going to finance your home, understanding what type of financing is available in the purchase price range you are considering will help you know what to expect when it is time to sell.

Some buyers will use cash, but most use financing. Take a close look at your individual situation with your CPA, then determine the best use of your cash and available credit. Realtors® aren't able to address all the financing options available by lenders of all sorts, but you should be presented with many of the main options as well as some unique programs that could be a good fit for you.

> The most important point I can make here is that contacting me directly is important so that I can put you on track for finding nothing but the BEST financing for your needs. I have had years of experience in being a loan officer, so I can help direct you to a professional lender with an on-time lending history that'll assist you and your unique situation well. It's really difficult to do the search yourself online!

Some special programs are only available through specific lenders, while others are available from most mortgage lenders. Discuss up front what makes these programs unique, and who specifically would be interested in the program. Qualifying guidelines vary a bit depending on the "lender's overlay" to the program itself. For example, while a VA (Veterans Affairs loan) may not have a specific credit score requirement, the specific lender may overlay their requirement so that the buyer will need a 620 FICO score. Checking with the lender of choice about their individual requirements is the best starting place. Rates can have such a huge impact on payments and qualification issues. Don Hogan, a local loan officer with Northpoint Bank stated:

> Obviously, everybody knows that interest rates will affect payments. When rates go up, payments go up and vice versa. Most people don't know exactly what it means on a qualification basis and how rates can affect purchasing power. For instance, take a VA loan for $350,000 at a rate of 4% on a 30-year fixed loan. This would have a principal and interest payment of $1670.95. If the rate were to increase to 4.50%, that payment would be $1773.40, over $100 per month more and over $6000 more over 5 years. That .50% rate increase means that a borrower would need to earn over $4200 per year to maintain the same debt ratio. If the ratios are tight then it could mean having to look for a lower priced home.

I am going to go through a few of the loan programs available. I'll give a brief intro to the loans so you know which programs best fit your needs.

The following is best suited for you if you have low cash available for purchasing your new home. Gifts from family are allowed.

FEDERAL HOUSING ADMINISTRATION LOAN (FHA)

This program is a government insured loan that came into existence in 1934. FHA insures mortgages on single family and multifamily homes including manufactured homes. FHA doesn't lend money but provides lenders with mortgage insurance protection against losses. Approved lenders underwrite the loan to FHA guidelines. Upfront MIP is usually added to the loan amount and is 1.75% (can change) of the loan. Monthly mortgage insurance (MI) is collected with the mortgage payment. FHA loan amount limits for El Paso County for a one living-unit property is $393,300

The advantages to using the FHA program:

1. Low down payment requirement. Currently around 3.5%.
2. Closing costs can be paid by the seller, builder, agent, or gifted by a relative.
3. Down payment can be gifted by a relative

Property condition requirements are a bit more difficult than that of a conventional mortgage. An approved FHA appraiser will determine if the property meets the minimum FHA standards. This appraisal inspection is not a home inspection and is very limited in nature. If the property is in poor condition, the seller may not want to accept an FHA offer since the minimum condition requirement will come into play and require that the property be brought up to that minimum standard. The buyer can back out of the transaction if the seller will not make the necessary repairs. This weakens the offer upfront on houses that need work. I will help you determine if the property meets the standards with the best educated overview I can make (without being an inspector).

There is an FHA product that can save the deal, the 203k FHA loan, which I will discuss next.

203K FHA LOAN PROGRAM

Don Hogan with Northpointe Bank stated:

> The 203K program is a government insured home loan that allows a buyer to get into a home that may not be completely suitable for them or needs repairs to bring it up to FHA standards. It can be done either at time of purchase or as a refinance.
>
> Many types of improvements are allowed; from structural repairs, to energy conservation improvements and installing kitchen appliances. Luxury items are really the only prohibition.
>
> There are two types of 203(k) programs: Standard and Limited.
>
> The Standard option is used for more extensive work as it has a minimum repair/renovation amount of $5000 and can go as high as the county limit for FHA loans. The standard option requires a HUD consultant to manage the project. The limited option has no minimum but has a maximum repair/renovation amount of $35,000. There is no HUD consultant required for the limited option but may be used.
>
> Work must be completed by a licensed contractor and there must be an arms-length relationship between a borrower and the contractor. All work must be completed within six months from the settlement of the loan.

The next program is for Veterans, either active or honorably discharged, that have their certificate of eligibility available.

VETERANS AFFAIR LOAN (VA)

A VA loan is a mortgage loan that is guaranteed by the U.S. Department of Veterans Affairs. Most mortgage lenders can do a VA loan. The original Servicemen's Readjustment Act, passed by the U.S. Congress in 1944, extended a large amount of benefits to eligible veterans. In 1970 and 1992, this act was amended to become the benefit program we know today. The VA loan limit guaranty is $453,100 for most VA loans. (Please remember that this amount varies by area and can change over time, so please contact me for the latest information.)

No down payment is required under the program and closing costs can be paid for by the seller, lender, or gifted by a relative. The loan allows veterans to borrow up to 103.3% of the purchase price or certificate of reasonable value, whichever is less.

There is a VA funding fee that can be added to the loan upfront. For a 0% down loan, the fee is 2.15% for the first use. The fee goes up for additional uses. The fee can be waived based on disability status of the veteran borrower.

There are obvious benefits to this type of loan. No money down, and seller-paid closing costs mean that the veteran can have no money out of pocket after closing to buy a house. The interest rate is competitive with the market rates. There are also some very creative lenders who will allow for credit card reduction and will pay the closing costs for the client. You do have to be eligible for this loan.

> Go to my website at brokerdarren.com/vendors to apply for a loan or get additional details.

Can you have more than one VA loan at a time? The answer is *yes,* but the total amount you qualify for will not go over the maximum. Again, you will need to speak directly with a lender to get additional details. The VA loan program is not an investor loan, so finding out the details will help assess what is the best approach for your financing needs.

Can a VA loan be used to purchase a manufactured house? The answer is yes, in some cases. The home needs to be a HUD approved home that has only been located on the property to be purchased. In other words, it couldn't have been moved from a mobile home park and onto a lot and qualify. A foundation engineer will also need to approve the foundation and tiedown system for the home. So, if you are interested in purchasing a manufactured house, even on acreage, you will want to call me and see if the home itself qualifies. I have sold many manufactured houses to veterans and it can be an excellent option for you to consider.

The Conventional programs mentioned next are for a buyer that has at least 3% down, a good credit score, and some money in the bank. Each conventional program has its own qualification guidelines along with cash in the bank guidelines. Good credit scores will benefit you the most with conventional financing.

CONVENTIONAL LOAN

There are many conventional loan programs available including a 97% loan to value program that gives FHA a run for its money. Qualifying guidelines vary based on the programs but are usually a bit more difficult to qualify for than the government programs. Rates across all programs vary based on your FICO score. The maximum, conforming loan amount in Colorado Springs is currently $548,250 for a single unit property. Anything over this amount is considered a jumbo loan and typically has a higher interest rate.

There are many variations on conventional loan programs. Banks with their own investors can make their own rules on loans they intend on servicing. Stated income programs are making a comeback (for the self-employed, mainly), and many other programs are available. Speak with your lender directly about which program suites your individual needs.

The following programs are best suited for purchasers who aren't quite ready to buy but would like to secure the current prices before they go up with appreciation and demand. Low fico scores (580 and above) and other issues affecting qualifying for a normal loan make these programs attractive.

LEASE WITH OPTION TO PURCHASE PROGRAMS

Visit www.brokerdarren.com/leaseoption for additional details about these programs.

Home Partners of America

This program is a lease with option to purchase for one year at a time. They will let you choose a house you wish to buy (they approve the property), they purchase the property and lease it out to you with an option to purchase the home in one year. You can renew the lease up to five years.

The person that this program works for is someone who wants to buy but cannot purchase today due to financial or personal obstacles. Typical obstacles to purchasing may be bankruptcy, divorce, medical expenses, loss of job, needing time to sell a currently owned home, or having been denied for a mortgage (and other reasons). There are many restrictions to the property, one being the price must be between $100,000 and $550000 with a minimum of two bedrooms. Home Partners website has many listed properties that they will approve for purchase. Visit their website at www.homepartners.com for additional details. Make sure to let them know who your Realtor® is as they assist you.

The difficulty with the program is that the monthly rent and right to purchase go up year to year. The monthly rent has a 3.75% yearly increase and the right to purchase option goes up 5% based on the purchase price of the property. For example, if Home Partners buys a house and you lease it at a purchase price of $300,000, after the first year the purchase price would be $315,000

My opinion on this program: it is very limited in nature for the buyer. If appreciation goes up in the neighborhood you are looking to purchase, then the 5% increase is covered. Rent increases are high so you won't want to be in the lease for very long. This does let you "test the water" in experiencing living in the area and lets you secure a home you like now before prices go up. You really don't lose if you back out of the lease when it comes up for renewal so if there is a house you like better for a better price—I can get you into that house instead of you staying in the lease. You still must qualify for the program, so getting started on that process is essential up front.

Trio

This program is newer to Colorado, and our office is one of the first to use the program. There are many benefits to this program, so let's take a quick look at some of the details:

- No down payment required.
- Earn home equity before you buy.
- Invest in your future—no more renting houses.
- Home ownership tools and counseling included.
- More details can be found at www.thinktrio.com

Some of the program requirements include:

- 580+ minimum credit score.
- $3600 month household income. Trio will consider side jobs as income.
- Payment cannot exceed 1/3 of your household income.
- 24+ month housing history a plus.
- 2+ months saving ($4000 minimum).

- 50% maximum debt-to-income ratio.

The steps involved in the process:

- Apply
- Pre-qualify
- Find a home (my job), usually not older than 10 years
- Make the offer, get it accepted
- Final approval
- Sign the lease option, make the required deposits
- Make first payment, close, move in
- Buy when ready

Trio has two primary programs: a 3-year lease option and a 1-5-year lease option.

My opinion on this program: it suits a very limited number of clients. If your credit score is too low but above 580, or if you don't have enough money for an FHA down payment and you don't have VA eligibility then this program may work well for you. It gives you time and you accumulate the appreciation on the property so when you finance it you should have enough equity to not have much out of pocket when you purchase it. You can walk away at the end of the lease, but you will be subject to a fee (under $1000) and must pay for any damage you did to the property while it was yours.

If you don't have enough funds to close a loan and FHA limits are okay for you, then we may consider on of these programs that can help with cash to close needed when you purchase a home.

DOWN PAYMENT ASSISTANCE PROGRAMS AND GRANT PROGRAMS

CHFA (two programs available) is a program that helps with the down payment. There are city grant programs and bank programs that all help with down payments and closing costs. The availability of these programs varies, so a call to the local lender would be in order to see if one is available that fits your needs. Commonly, these programs all have purchase price limits and income limits.

Investors that don't qualify for conventional financing and are looking at other sources can use hard money lenders.

Hard Money Lenders

This is a category of lending that has wide-open criteria. Typically, hard money lenders fund loans for investors. The terms of the loans are usually short with a high front-end fee (discount points). Locally, Pine Financial is one of the predominant players in the hard money market. They have great programs for investors that allow you to purchase a property and do renovations at a relatively high loan-to-value. www.pinefinancialgroup.com is the website you will want to visit to check out their programs and how they work. They also sponsor some great training events for the investor, so make sure and check out the schedule of their training and attend what events center on your plan for investing. Make sure to sign up for their newsletter. I will be writing a short book on investing soon, so check back often on my website.

Next is an interview with a loan officer that I respect. She includes her professional input on lending in our current market.

INTERVIEW WITH A LOAN OFFICER
Shelly Shelly, Integrity Mortgage Inc.

Tell me about your experience in the mortgage industry.

For 18 years I have helped people achieve their dream of becoming a homeowner. Through my years of experience, I have learned two of the most important aspects to purchasing a home 1) Use a reputable lender and 2) Communication is key. On a personal level I love everything outdoors: hiking, fishing, biking and spending quality time with my two young boys and husband.

How long has the company you are currently working for been in business and what makes them great to work for?

President and CEO, Russell Rowe, founded Integrity Mortgage Inc. in 2002. With many years in the financial industry, Russell has taken the Integrity Team to one of the leading mortgage firms in Colorado Springs. With us, you will always find honesty, loyalty, respect and genuine attention from all aspects in the home buying process.

What is your differential advantage? Why would you be the best loan officer for the job?

A few things that I feel set me apart is my knowledge and experience, which is one of the most important things when searching for a lender. A few other things that separate me from other loan officers is that I am available- I am here to help after work hours and on weekends with excellent customer service skills and communication. Clients have also mentioned to me that

I am personable, and I will go through options so they can pick what loan is best for their family. Some loan officers will just say *Hey: this is the loan you should do.* I care and I will discuss the pros and cons of the different loan programs, not just tell you what to do.

What are the most common issues you see today with buyers qualifying for a mortgage?

Right now, I would say low inventory of homes that are available in lower price points. When I work with first-time homebuyers, they don't have many homes to choose from and it is very competitive… Sometimes we want to entertain looking at new construction and the prices are too high and not affordable for every buyer.

If a client can't qualify today, do you help advise them what they need to do to qualify in the future? What and how?

I most certainly do; I work with some clients for years before they buy a home. Biggest thing buyers need help with is getting their credit reports cleaned up and raising the credit scores. Another big thing is they just need to save more money.

What loan program do you use the most in Colorado Springs?

I honestly do a mix of everything. When I looked at my numbers for 2020 I had 60% government loans: VA/USDA/FHA and 40% Conventional.

What is one of the most unique loans you offer to your customers?

USDA: it's a loan that allows you to do 100% financing (No Down Payment) and the PMI is almost ½ the cost compared to FHA.

Do you see interest rates increasing soon in the future? Why or why not?

The consensus among four industry experts is that mortgage rates are likely to rise from the current low of 2.67%, but they don't expect a massive spike. Most experts are forecasting rates to stay close to their current historic lows early in the year and maybe rise as high as 3.4% by the end of 2021.

Likewise, home prices should continue to grow, although none of the experts are predicting growth as fast as this year's. Instead, they expect median home prices to rise a maximum of 6%. The strongest price growth is likely during the first half of 2021, before moderating later on.

The vaccine approval and initial distribution of the first COVID-19 can provide a much-needed boost to the economy. The new stimulus package can help spur economic growth, helping to push interest rates higher in the long run. A continued economic recovery coupled with increased government spending will place upward pressure on mortgage rates.

It's forecasted that interest rates won't rise significantly until the second half of 2021, after the COVID vaccine has been widely administered and the economy starts making a more sustained recovery.

Based on the logistics of the vaccine distribution that have been made public, It could take 6-to-8 months for the vaccine to reach a majority of the population, delaying any positive economic effects until late in the year.

SHELLEY SHELLEY
INTEGRITY MORTGAGE & FINANCIAL

Website: www.integritymtg.com/staff-member/shelley-v-shelley
Email: shelley.shelley@integritymtg.com
Facebook: integritymortgageinc

To learn more about some of the area's best lenders visit my website at www.brokerdarren.com/vendors.

THE FRONT YARD SEMI-TRUCKS

A UNIQUE CELEBRATION FOR HOME OWNERSHIP!

One of the most rewarding parts of mortgage lending is having the opportunity to watch your client's dreams come true. As a lender my territory included California City, CA. This little town was near Edwards Air Force

Base and was expanding at the time because of the en-listed military growth. One of the agents I worked with regularly sent referrals to me.

I contacted the referred client and had to have a Spanish translator help me. This buyer and his family owned a trucking business and were amazing, hard-working people. I completed the loan and the buyer was over-joyed. He sent his two brothers to me and when it was all said and done, I helped three families realize their home ownership dreams.

In appreciation for the agent and my work, we were in-vited to a big BBQ in our honor. How cool is that?! We showed up expecting a small family group. I believe there were probably 80 people there, most of which did not speak English. Two huge semis were in the front yard and granny came up and gave me a big hug. People showed us such love and appreciation, even though I do not know what they said most of the time due to the language bar-rier. I believe it was all good, though. I tried foods that were not familiar to me, but it all tasted amazing. To be appreciated like that really warmed my heart.

THE CREDIT CLEANING INDUSTRY

So, what is credit cleaning? Why in the world would anyone need it? Of course, the answer is the all mighty credit score that is used in your qualification for a loan. There is a minimum credit score for most financing and an optimum credit score that will get you the best terms. If your credit score doesn't reach these numbers, then it might be time for credit cleaning. Companies that specialize in helping you work with the credit reporting bureaus to remove or correct items that are misreported are called "credit cleaning companies." The in-dustry has gone through many changes and there are very few profes-sional companies helping customers clean up their credit.

In the past, there were many fly-by-night companies that didn't get results and charged way too much for what they did. Over the years, I've experienced many different approaches to cleaning up credit and some of those approaches work, and some don't. Recently, I've been very impressed with a company, Riverstone Law, (www.riverstonelaw.com), and the programs they offer. Many lenders have their favorites with whom they have had good success.

Yes, it can be an expense, but well worth it. You will need to work with the company and make sure that you do as they say. The three credit bureaus work differently where it comes to reporting your credit. Creditors also don't necessarily report to all three bureaus so the score can vary dependent on which bureaus the finance company uses. Typically for a mortgage loan, a lender will pull a merged report that pulls from all three bureaus.

Most credit cleaning companies use the fact that your credit may be, and usually is, incorrect. The reporting agencies either must correct the problem or completely remove it. It costs more than it is worth, in most cases, for the company to get it done in a timely fashion, so the improper item gets removed from the report. I have witnessed cases where the credit score goes up over 100 points after the credit cleaning is complete. This can take anywhere from three months to a year, depending on the complexity of the items and how many items are needing correction.

If you end up in a situation where your credit score is very close to the required score, the lender may make suggestions that will have enough of an impact to raise your score enough to get the financing done. Don't assume that paying credit off raises your score since often the opposite is created. Once that you enter the process of getting pre-approved with a lender you will know what process will work for you. Sometimes you need to take on a small credit card and pay it off every month. Other times it will be much more complex. Realize that the lender is attempting to reduce risk by setting specific guidelines on credit score.

There are items that credit cleaning can't resolve. Some include IRS liens, child support liens, unpaid collection accounts, and recent foreclosures. These things can keep you from getting a loan right now. Don't assume anything until you have met with a reputable lender and talked through it all.

CHAPTER 3:
General Steps in the Real Estate Transaction

THIS CHAPTER WILL REVIEW THE STEPS INVOLVED in the purchase process for all types of real estate acquisition. This is just the general list of the items that will be completed through the real estate transaction. This list is not a complete list, but will give you a roadmap for the process to home ownership. I believe it is important to understand the process and hire a Realtor® that will handle this process with your best interests in mind. For a more detailed list, go to www.brokerdarren.com/transaction.

- **Find a competent, caring real estate expert.** Choose a real estate professional that has successfully completed transactions in the type of real estate you are purchasing and cares about your unique situation. Visit www.

 for additional information about my experience.

- **Identify your purpose in purchasing real estate.** Are you buying a house as a primary residence or strictly as an investment? How long will you keep the property? Are you considering new construction or re-sale or land? Are you an investor (every purchase should be evaluated as an investment) with the purpose of being a landlord?

- **Write down your detailed "dream home list."** Consider property amenities, area amenities, view requirements, school districts you would like to be in, type of property (single family, townhouse, etc.)—as many features you can list.

- **Which type of financing will be best for your purchase?** Get qualified for that financing. See my list of preferred lenders at www.brokerdarren.com/vendors. The type of financing you choose can restrict the house that you are able to buy. There are many different loan programs (see chapter 2 on Loan Programs) so don't assume you know what is best. In order to make an offer in the current market you need to have a pre-approval issued by a local lender. This process will not only advise you on the loan programs that are best for you but will also let you know estimates of payments so that you can choose a payment you are comfortable with and that will determine the purchase price you'll be targeting.

- **Let your real estate professional go through your "dream home list" and put together an automated search directly through the Multiple Listing Service (MLS).** This will set you up on your own customized website that will display listings that are active that meet your criteria. This website will update daily with new listings and pull under-contract listings off the site. You can save your favorites so that they can be viewed by your agent.

- **View properties and analyze them based on your needs and wants.**

- Select your property.

- Run comparable checks on recent sales activity and prepare offer.

- Deliver offer with pre-approval letter from your lender.

- Offer accepted!

- Delivery of earnest money.

- Inspection scheduled.

- Disclosures reviewed and approved.

- Association documents reviewed and approved.

- Title documents reviewed and approved.

- Insurance for home put in place and approved by you.

- Inspection performed.

- Inspection objection sent to seller.

- Inspection resolution agreed to and signed.

- Due diligence documents delivered and reviewed and approved by buyer.

- Survey or ILC performed and approved by the buyer and/or title company and lender (if required).

- All loan conditions met for final approval.

- Appraisal completed, at value, no work requirements.

- Final complete loan approval, clear to close.

- Closing scheduled.

- Final walk-through completed.

- Closing, usually at title company.

- All required funds in certified funds delivered to closer.

- Documents signed and loan funding completed.

- Closing, keys delivered with all remotes to garage etc. to buyer.

CHAPTER 4:
Important Transaction Details

THE OFFER

The moment has finally arrived, and you are ready to write an offer. This is what we have worked so hard to achieve. 2020 and 2021 is showing us that the market is still a sellers' market. What this means to you is that you will need to select the property, write the offer, and submit it as quickly as possible since you'll be most likely competing with other buyers. This is difficult for most buyers since they don't want to be pressured in any way with the biggest purchase they may make in their life.

The fact exists: "if you snooze, you lose." I really hate to say it so directly, but my job is to get my clients the best house that fits their needs, at the best price possible, with the best terms, and in a timeline that works for them. In a sellers' market this can be a tall order. **But being prepared is the key.** Knowing the type of property, location including desired school districts, condition that is acceptable, and making sure your financing in order is all required to go out and view properties so that if you find one, these things are checked off on our list.

Here is a brief list of how we will work through the offer. (Note that the following is specific to the buyer services I offer, and how I help my clients. This can vary between agents, and I can only speak to how *I* handle offers and represent my clients.)

1. After the Market Analysis is completed, an offer price will be discussed based on property condition, days on the market, and how closely the house meets your needs.

2. I will contact your lender and get a price specific pre-approval letter to provide with your offer. The type of financing, down payments, etc. affect how the seller will view your offer. (I will discuss this with you in the very beginning of the process.)

3. We will go through all the contingencies and dates on the offer so that you understand the implications of them all.

4. There are many strategies that I use to make your offer as attractive as possible to the seller. The "devil is in the details" can be true with a large contract like we use for real estate. The seller's agent, if doing their job, will look at all the fine details and implications on all the areas of the contract for their seller. I know our contracts well and will suggest how we can adjust details in our contract that can make our offer more attractive, as needed, so that your offer gets accepted. We will discuss how all of this impacts you, and based on the competitiveness of the property, we will do what it takes to get your offer accepted as long as you are protected and understand all the implications. **I work for you and your interests.**

5. If the offer is countered, we will consider the counter to make sure that you understand all of the implications before you accept the counter, or decide to move on. I use the "peace maker strategy" in my negotiations. I believe that presenting our offer position with supporting,

relevent information in a friendly, non-threatening voice and posture, giving my buyers the best chance at getting their offers accepted.

6. Once that we have an accepted offer, our timeline (that was laid out in the contract) begins. I will need to submit the earnest money negotiated on the contract to the listing agent or title company to meet the dates specified. You will get with your lender, and then it all gets going!

WHAT IS EARNEST MONEY?

One of the most misunderstood items on the contract is earnest money. Earnest money has also been called a deposit by many buyers. So, what is it?

Earnest money is money that is given with the contract to show the seller the serious intention of the buyer to buy the house. Earnest money is not a down payment even though it can be used for this at closing. This amount, typically 1% of the sales price, gets deposited into an escrow holder's account. The escrow holder can be a listing agency, title company, or other party that has an escrow account legally set up for holding earnest money. The escrow holder may not touch or use the money in any way during or after the transaction unless instructions are provided by both the buyer and seller instructing them to do so. This money does not belong to the seller unless the buyer is in default and an earnest money release form is executed by buyer and seller. There are other rules that apply and can vary from state to state.

What earnest money is *not*: it is usually not a non-refundable amount just given to the seller. There are strings attached to this earnest deposit, specified in the contract, usually including inspection termination, appraisal issues, loan approval, title objections, and more. The contract has a date table that specifies when each one of these items need to be completed and approved. If the buyer does not approve of one of them, then the contract can be terminated, and the earnest money returned to the buyer.

What happens to the earnest money when the house closes? That is determined by the buyer. The buyer, working with a competent lender, would decide if he gets the money back, applies it to the down payment or applies it to closing costs. The seller does not just get the earnest money on top of the sales price unless the contract states so.

When does the seller get to keep the earnest money? Typically, if the buyer is in default and has passed all objection deadlines and still does not complete the transaction, then the seller gets to keep the money. I have only had this happen a couple of times in my career, and in both cases the buyer knew they were in default and they gave up the earnest money with complete understanding of how it happened. "Cold feet" at the end of the transaction will usually result in the buyer giving up the earnest money to the seller.

You notice that I say typically when I speak of the details of earnest money. This is because you can specify if you want to do something different with the earnest money. In a sellers' market, like it is here in Colorado Springs in 2021, there are times when a buyer will make the earnest money "non-refundable." *Why* you might ask? It makes the offer stronger to the seller since the seller knows that even if the buyer wants to back out, the earnest money is theirs. On occasion there may be a no-earnest-money transaction. This can occur in a buyers' market or when a buyer is low on cash but can still qualify for a loan. In a seller's market this does not normally occur.

The contract has an area to specify when the earnest money is to be delivered to the earnest holder. I have had this happen when the buyer is out of town and must mail the check to me or they have to transfer funds to have the money liquid. There is also a promissory note that can be executed for the earnest money, but this isn't used very often in a sellers' market. The earnest money normally can be a personal check, but the seller can specify if they want "good funds" (like a cashiers check).

Earnest money is different than a down payment. A down payment is an amount that will depend on the loan requirements you are getting, or your desires. Some loans require $0 down payment, but the buyer would still have to come up with the earnest money, normally.

INSPECTIONS

In the state of Colorado, home inspectors are not licensed… yet. It is critical for a Realtor® to do his homework regarding the home inspector that is chosen to do the inspection. We need to make sure the reputation of the inspector is good with our colleagues, that the services they offer are complete, and that the fees are reasonable. The buyer chooses the home inspector, but your real estate agent can recommend a few that they know and trust through experience.

Both the buyer and the agent will be with the home inspector during the entire inspection. This helps with interpretation of the findings of the home inspector. Once the report is written, it can be difficult to understand specifically what the inspector is referring to unless you were there during the inspection. Some of the general categories that an inspector reports on are:

- **Roof:** the inspector is not a roofer but is trained on what to look for regarding condition issues with the roof. If the inspector finds a problem, he will recommend that a roofer inspects the roof and suggests repairs.

> I use an inspection company that has a service, for an additional charge, that will estimate the cost of repairs and provide a report with that estimate.
> This is a very helpful service.

The inspector will look for building permits for an indication of when the roof was last replaced. Hail damage is somewhat easily noted and can be turned in to the owner's home insurance company for a claim. Timing can cause delays in closing if a claim is filed.

- **Siding:** the inspector will inspect the siding for obvious damage and will suggest repairs for what he finds. Stucco typically has very few problems where lap siding will have paint and sealing issues that lead to swelling and lack of performance of the siding.
- **Decks:** this is a highly involved inspection with most home inspectors. They will look for rotting wood supports, cracking and splitting wood, finishing issues on the wood, and general condition and structural issues with the deck.
- **Doors and windows:** on the exterior, the inspector looks for obvious problems such as breakage, cracks, door seals, handle and locking mechanisms, etc. Typically, the inspector looks for all issues on the outside of the house that can cause deterioration, lack of performance, water intrusion, and lack of proper function. Inside, the inspector will check for proper operation of all doors and windows and check for seal leakage in windows.
- **Interior heating and cooling:** the inspector will inspect the heating system, check for proper operation, Co2 leaks, proper burner operation, and general condition issues. The inspector will call for a cleaning and inspection by a licensed contractor if there are any issues.
- **Water heater:** age is always checked as well as burner operation and connections on the top of the water heater and the blow-off valve.
- **Appliances:** the inspector turns on the appliances and checks for proper operation.
- **Plumbing:** the inspector will check for obvious leaks under the sinks and with the exposed plumbing in the utility room. He cannot check behind the walls for any plumbing issues, but if anything is suspected, you can hire a professional to take a further look.
- **Electrical:** the inspector will pull the cover off the panel and check for double taps and proper installation of the wires in the panel. He will check the outlets for proper grounding and operation. He will make sure that CGFI's are installed where needed.

- **Radon:** most inspectors can perform a radon check and will usually drop off the digital detector 3 days prior to the inspection so it can be read at the inspection.
- Other inspection items can include sewer scope, mold investigation, and other site-specific items.

This is just a very general list to give you an idea of some of the items that will be looked at by a home inspector. Most home inspectors are very professional and produce an excellent report detailing all their findings for you and your agent to review. **You can expect to pay anywhere from $250 to $500 for your inspection depending on the house size.**

Here is where the inspection issues get real.

I know that the perception of most buyers is that a seller *must* perform the items that are requested on an inspection objection. Unfortunately in a sellers' market, we won't be able to get everything that we might want a seller to do based on the inspection items.

What is the best approach? Focus on the most important items that truly matter in the big picture of your purchase. Asses the most expensive items that really *should* be fixed to make the house marketable in the long run, and allow the home to be financed. Your agent can advise you on which inspection items are vital for the seller to fix.

Some inspection items affect the market value of a home, and once the seller is aware of the problem, they need to disclose it to the next buyer (should the deal fall apart). So, get it done now and move on.

After the inspection items are reviewed, an inspection objection needs to be put together and presented to the seller. Your inspection objection needs to be straight forward and clear. Just like the original contract, you must be a smart negotiator and know how to write up the objection well.

Here's an example of a situation that needs an inspection objection:

A buyer asks a seller to have a plumber replace the trap under the sink. The parts are a total of $10, but a plumber will charge a seller a call-out fee just to show up, let alone the charges for doing the actual work. A $10 repair has now turned into an over $100 expense.

A better alternative would be to ask that an affordable handyman replace the trap under the sink, or simple ask that it's replaced and not specify who does the job. To fix a faucet, you really don't need a plumber. So just make sense out of your requests, and make sure they feel reasonable for the seller. (Note, some items *must* have a contractor for repairs, including heating unit repairs, water heater repairs, roof repairs etc.)

There *is* a problem with the inspection process that I attempt to address using specific home inspectors. It's called "gaps," and it's what occurs between the home inspection and coverages with the home warranty. AMPRO Inspections (www.amproinspections.com) has warranties that cover the gaps. The inspectors check the appliances for recalls, and some can even provide a 5-year roof protection warranty (just to name a couple of their services). Check their website or link from my website at www. brokerdarren.com/vendors.

HOME WARRANTY CONSIDERATIONS

In the past, home warranties were a novelty and not something that was taken very seriously. With companies not really offering much with the warranty and pre-existing conditions killing most claims, the reputations of the companies suffered. Although pre-existing conditions still apply, the completeness of the home inspection helps prevent these problems from occurring, in most cases.

As with any warranty you would purchase, you need to review the coverages and exclusions in the policy. There are home warranties that are for new construction that extend the coverage the builder supplies for an additional 4 years. Basic policies from most providers can be as low as $295 and as high as $700 for new construction.

Most companies have around three plans available. Each plan upgrade covers more. A/C, refrigerator, toilets, etc. are usually not covered on a basic plan. Deductibles can be as low as $45 for each callout, or higher, depending on the company you choose.

The warranty companies schedule their approved contractors to come out and do the work. Some companies may let you choose the contractor, but that isn't typical.

So, is it worth it to purchase a home warranty? It really depends on the financial condition of the buyer (available resources to pay for work themselves), and how the buyer feels about warranties in general. I typically ask a buyer if they purchased an extended warranty for any vehicle they own and use this as a guide to discuss the purchase of a home warranty. Even though surprises can come up even with a home inspection, the risk is typically low if everything in the home was inspected prior to purchase and fixed as part of the purchase process. I will take the time to discuss the warranties available with you and you can make the decision if it is right for you. Please see the vendors section at my website for additional information at www.brokerdarren.com/vendors.

BAD INSULATION

THE *PATIO* DOESN'T NEED THAT...

There are many opinions about having a home inspection on a newly constructed home. I probably was sitting on the side of the fence that said there was really no purpose to having an inspection on a new home. The home would have been inspected by the building department during construction, so why have a separate inspection?

I was wrong.

I always present options to my buyers, and in this case, the buyer decided to have a home inspection on a new home he was building. The home was completed, and the inspector showed up for the inspection. The tract foreman pulled me aside and quipped, "boy is this a waste of time and money."

I agreed, but wanted to respect my clients' wishes. During the inspection, the inspector told the foreman that he would be cutting the wall joint tape around the attic access. The foreman was rather irritated and told my buyer that they would not be repairing the tape.

After a couple of minutes, the inspector called me to climb the ladder and investigate the attic. There was nice insulation everywhere and it all looked up to code. He pointed to an area without insulation and said that the area over a patio did not need it. He told me to go down and look at which side the patio the bedroom was on, because obviously... the bedroom DID need insulation.

Yep, the builder had put the insulation over the patio and *not* the bedroom. I told the foreman, and he huffed and puffed as he climbed the ladder to see it for himself. A humbled foreman and Realtor® were on site that day. The inspector was worth five times his fee. **I always suggest a home inspection now.**

CHAPTER 5:
Land

SITTING IN FRONT OF MY OFFICE at Cardinal, Realtors® in Tehachapi, CA was an old, red Jeep Cherokee. I loved this vehicle since it was four-wheel drive and ready to take on the mountains and trek across large, open lots that I enjoyed taking my customers to see.

Raw land has its appeal for buyers who want to realize the dream of building their own house. Sometimes it's just the dream of owning a piece of land to just sit on and have lunch. Whatever the dream, raw land still lights the fire of the imagination. Here in Colorado, it is a rare commodity. Builders are constantly buying the large parcels to subdivide and build housing subdivisions. Smaller builders buy the available, single parcels to build their customers dream homes. Custom builders buy lots one at a time to sell to a waiting buyer. Most available lots are remotely located, typically far from established neighborhoods and quite a drive to the closest large community. This may suit some that are looking for the tranquil life in remote locations.

Let's look first at why a buyer would consider buying land in the first place. This may seem obvious, yet I find many buyers do not stay consistent with the original reason they wanted to buy a wonderful piece of land in the first place. A few of those reasons would be:

1. ***Building your dream home***. This really is the number one reason that raw land is sold. I have had many calls with buyers looking to build a home over the years. Locating the "perfect" lot is the first step. A full analysis up front is important so that the budget and the dream match.
2. ***Planning on building a home in the future***. There are many buyers that just want to secure a lot so that their future dreams may be realized (potentially far into the future). It is a ton of fun to take a chair and pad of paper out on the lot and spend countless hours drawing out what it would look like to someday build that retirement home or vacation home.
3. ***Investing in a lot to resell or to subdivide and sell off individual parcels for profit.*** Subdividing is so much more difficult to accomplish than people understand, but I'll go into a bit of detail about this also.
4. ***Having a camping area to enjoy the great outdoors.*** Sometimes this can work and be lots of fun. But checking the local ordinances and CC&Rs (covenants, conditions, and restrictions) for the lot sometimes reveals that you can't do it.
5. ***Developing commercially.*** I won't cover much on this in this book but look for additional resources to follow.

No matter the reason for buying a lot, there are many items to look at. Home building is covered in a different chapter, so I want to take you through the general process of looking at a lot, evaluating the lot, and deciding which one meets your needs.

CHOOSING YOUR LAND

Once that you have decided on an area that has vacant lots available for sale in your price range, you will want to select a few to view. Before your visit, make sure to check out the area's restrictions

Covenants, Conditions and Restrictions and Associations

Review all documents that restrict the use of the land. CC&Rs are very common and lay out the use of the area where the lot is located. Association documents review is critical. Check on the financial status of the association, minutes of the meetings (which may indicate what type of problems area owners are facing) and all the restrictions in the area. A professional is needed to help in this analysis. An experienced real estate broker that has sold many lots would be a good choice.

Once you review the restrictions, make a list of items that you want to identify and utilize my list at www.brokerdarren.com/land before you head out to the location.

The view

Look around. Do you like what you see? Is there a suitable location not far from the road to locate your new home that takes advantage of the view? Are there potential builders or houses that can be built in the future that would obscure your view? Try to look at the whole picture when considering the view and the cost to build on a spot that would have the best view. A long driveway can cost more money as well as the cost to install utilities further away from the connection point. The view has a big impact on the value and future resale of the lot and any improvements placed on it.

Weeds and foliage

You will want to review what weeds and foliage exist on the lot and if they are toxic or not. You don't want to lose a pet due to it chewing on a plant that is poisonous. At the very least, you want to know about the problem so that you can mitigate it. Clearing the lot away from a new structure can be very important for fire mitigation. This link has some great information about weeds and natural grasses in Colorado: www.colorado.gov/pacific/agconservation/noxious-weed-species

Local animal life

Small coyotes are known for taking a cat or small dog—let alone a mountain lion, hawk, owl, etc. Look for evidence of animal activity on the lot. Here is a list of potential animals that you may need to be concerned with: coloradosprings.gov/office-emergency-management/page/living-wildlife

Natural water flow

Can you see natural water flow through the lot that would affect where you want to place the house or other structures? Are curbs and gutters in the development? Take a good look at the slope of the land to see where it's possible for you to. You can save tons of money on grading and water diversion later. A water information guide can be found here: www.colorado.gov/pacific/sites/default/files/Citizen%27s%20Guide%20to%20Colorado%20Water%20Law.pdf

Fencing

Look for encroachments by neighbors onto this lot, or where this lot might encroach on another lot. What is the condition of the fences? All wood fences deteriorate quickly and the cost to replace can be very high. If you need fencing for animals or privacy, go to the local home improvement company to check on prices. A general guide about fence pricing can be found here: www.landscapingnetwork.com/fencing/cost.html

Environmental issues

Look for odd looking colors on the soil. Has someone been using the lot to dump chemicals or trash? A Phase I and Phase II environmental study would be a great idea if there is any indication of problems on the lot. This guide can help with explaining the study: dnr.wi.gov/files/pdf/pubs/am/am465.pdf Look for indications of problems. If the lot is in a developed community, talk with the neighbors about it. Ask if they have seen anyone entering onto the lot and dumping anything on it.

Neighbors

How do the neighbors care for their lot? Is there tons of trash, old cars, or other items that might be of concern? Have any buildings or sheds been built over the property line? Are there barking dogs or animals of concern?

Flight patterns

Look up and watch the skies. Are there a high number of aircraft arriving or departing from an airport? How do you feel about the sounds of airplanes flying overhead every hour? Flight pattern maps can be obtained here: https://www.faa.gov/airports/environmental/airport_noise/noise_exposure_maps/

Flood plain and erosion issues

Is the lot in a 100-year flood plain? Additional flood insurance will be required if it is. Here is where you can check msc.fema.gov/portal/home Look for obvious erosion patterns. Is there water flow from an adjacent parcel onto this parcel? If so, you may have additional issues to control the water flow.

Mining problems

Is the lot located near the mountains to the west of Colorado Springs? If so, you will want to check the mining map to see if the lot sits on a site where there is an underground mine shaft. Chemicals and soil collapse risk can be high. Look here for the map: coloradogeological-survey.org/geologic-hazards/subsidence-mine/maps/

Tree issues

Is the lot filled with trees? What are the restrictions for removing them if needed to clear for a building pad? Pine beetles are a major concern for pine trees. You can have an expert evaluate the trees for infestations. Follow this link for additional information: frarborists. com/services/beetle-prevention/

Expansive soils

The Colorado Springs area is known for having expansive soils. The soils are like a sponge and when water soaks the soil, it expands due to clay. Here is a great site to learn more about expansive soils and their effect: geology.com/articles/expansive-soil.shtml

Radon

Just about everywhere in El Paso county there is radon escaping the ground. When you build a house, this radon is trapped beneath the house and enters the house through the lower level. This gas is dangerous and can cause many health problems. Thankfully, there are solutions that aren't very costly, and the test is very simple. Learn more here www.elpasocountyhealth.org/services/radon For an example of a solution to a radon problem, check out this website-: aspenradon.com

You won't be able to test for radon before building a house, but make sure to budget for it. Typically, it is around $1500 for a basic system. If you build the system into the house during construction, the system will not be visible from the outside.

Utility connection costs

These costs can be reasonable or absolutely break the bank. For example, utility companies that have limited ability to process waste charge a huge amount to connect to the sewer line. The length of run from the street to the house makes a big difference in cost also. The type of obstacles to build around or through boulders can increase the cost. Occasionally these costs can be high enough to justify finding another lot. When the lot is in a developed area, it is straight forward finding out the connection costs. If water and sewer is not available, then drilling a well and installing a septic system will be the process of choice.

Keep in mind there are alternatives to all utilities. Off-the-grid properties (not connected to any power, water or sewer provider) can use a system that includes wind power generation, battery backup, generator power, and solar power. These methods of producing electricity can be very expensive up front, but beneficial for sustainability in the long run. Take a look at some of these alternatives here: www.energy.gov/energysaver/buying-and-making-electricity/planning-home-renewable-energy-systems

Water sources

The typical way to provide water to a house without a local source is through a well. Other options such as a water tank (water is tanked into your location) are expensive and usually only considered when no other option exists. Calling a well company is an important step before purchasing a lot to find out how deep the well will probably have to be, and any associated costs with the well installation. The well permit is obtained by the well company and will specify the use that you are requesting. Here is the state division of water resources link for additional information about wells: www.colorado.gov/pacific/sites/default/files/wellpermitguide_1.pdf

Use of water from a stream or small pond is very regulated in Colorado. The above website will give you additional information about water rights and usages in Colorado. Just because it is located on the lot doesn't mean you can use it.

Septic systems

The septic system size and type is regulated by the local health department for the area. The tank size is usually based on the number of bedrooms since this is related to the number of people using the system. Here is an excellent website that describes the different types of systems: https://www.epa.gov/septic/types-septic-systems El Paso County requires that the system is pumped and certified when the property is sold. Know at this step, if you are buying a rural lot, you will probably have to have a septic system.

Landslide susceptibility

This website will show you an analysis of landslide predictions for the Colorado Springs area: www.arcgis.com/apps/webappviewer/index.html

BUYING YOUR LAND

I realize there is much information to consider when looking at purchasing a lot. Even if you don't plan to build, you should look at these factors since they influence the value of the lot and the re-sale value. So, how much do lots cost today in the Colorado Springs, Colorado area? Let's look at some size and price analyses.

As of January 1, 2021, the following land statistics apply for the Pikes Peak Association of Realtors®:

- Total Lot listings in the MLS (Pikes Peak): 1315 active land listings
- 144 residential lot listings zoned R and all extensions for residential
- Active in Colorado Springs: 125 listings
- 5+ acres, 520 listings
- As an example, a 5-acre lot in Redtail Ranch in the Springs is listed for $250,000.
- Another example would be a 40-acre lot in Calhan listed for $44,000.

Obviously, location makes all the difference. Many lots are very difficult to build on or have utilities far from the lot. Looking at value and sales price and cost to improve is critical when considering any lot, as mentioned above.

JUST A MINUTE WHILE I SHOOT THIS BOAR

SELLING LAND IN THE MOUNTAINS

I have always enjoyed selling land. There is so much more to the process, and educating my buyer on all of the ins and outs of land considerations is very satisfying for me as I help them through the process.

One day I received a call from a new client that was referred to me, about going up into the south mountains of Tehachapi and look at some 20 acre lots. Now, these lots were *steep,* and a steep dirt road took us up to ride along the upper portion of the 5 to 20-acre parcels. Building a house on one of these lots would have been an expensive proposition.

I met the customer at the entrance to the area and he suggested that he take me up the hill since he had a great 4x4 Jeep. I agreed.

Off we went up into the mountains. It was beautiful, but again... *steep.* We had some discussions about why he wanted one of these lots and he stated that he wanted to hunt on it, *not* build a house.

Huh, well sounded good to me. We got out of the car and attempted to determine the lot boundaries which was difficult since there were no survey markers. Suddenly, I hear him take off back towards the Jeep. Of course, I first think to myself *great, he's decided to abandon me on top of this mountain.*

But no. He was digging in the back of the Jeep for something. He busted up and started running down the mountain. I looked closely and noted what he had been scrounging for in the back of the Jeep: his compound bow and arrows.

He disappeared for 30 minutes or so (that was a long 30 minutes) and suddenly appeared, out of breath.

"Well, I *almost* got me one" he stated, panting, and sweat dripping off his forehead. "You look like I was gonna leave you or something."

He stated how sorry he was, but he saw one of the largest boars he had ever seen.

"You don't have to have a license to hunt one of these, you know?" he stated.

I told him directly, "maybe not, but you *do* have to have the owner's permission since you don't eactly own this land yet!"

That concluded our adventure, and strangly, I never heard back from him.

CHAPTER 6:
Re-Sale Homes

MOST OF MY CAREER HAS BEEN OCCUPIED SELLING RE-SALE HOMES. I have sold manufactured homes, small ranch homes, huge multi-level homes, off-the-grid homes, multi-unit homes, condos and townhouses,… you name it, I've sold it. I have worked with HUD owned homes, VA properties, bank owned properties, auction houses and regular sales. I thought it would be a great idea to go through the process and all the considerations that happen when I help a buyer select a property.

There is much more that is involved than most people think. This book is about providing great information for you, the buyer, to use on your journey of buying a home. Customizing the journey to meet your specific needs is what I specialize in and look forward to the most.

Initially, I would like to summarize the real estate purchasing process in a simple, orderly way, and then go into the vital details that make up a successful transaction.

LOAN PRE-APPROVAL

The reason I put this section here is so that you can understand the importance of getting your financial affairs in order. Yes, it seems obvious, but I run into more problems associated with financing than any other issues in the sale of a home. You notice I didn't say *pre-qualification*. In a sellers' market, your offer needs to be strong and a *full* pre-approval needs to be in place and a letter issued from your lender stating what's been specifically looked at at the time of issuing this letter. It's important to make sure that you know what payments you will have when considering a specific price point, how much down payment is required, and what the closing costs will be for your own preparation, as well as whether or not we will ask the seller to pay them.

If you don't have any connections with a lender, my website lists several that I know personally and that can get the job done in a professional manner. Please visit my website at www.brokerdarren.com/vendors for my list of lenders.

> I will work closely with your lender so that I can request the lender letter to match our offer exactly. We don't ever tip our hand with letting a seller know how much you can qualify for—which is just a part of the expert negotiating skills I can bring.

OUR FIRST MEETING

How exciting! I always get excited when I get to assist a buyer in locating a home they have been dreaming of. Usually at this point, we have already spoken on the phone, and you have been through the pre-approval process to know how much you want to spend and what you qualify for.

First, we'll fill out a detailed questionnaire about what you are considering when looking at a new home. We will narrow down what matters most to you as well as review the different types of transactions we may be a part of: buying a re-sale home, building with a tract builder, custom home, or starting with a lot. We will identify what process works best for what your plans are. Once we decide, we fill out the detailed Property Identification Worksheet. I ask you lots of questions so that I can supply a list of available properties or builders that meet your criteria. What kind of properties will we be discussing? Let's look at a few next.

Types of properties available for your consideration in Colorado Springs:

TOWNHOUSES

If affordability and ease of maintenance on the outside of the home is important to you, then this may be an option.

Townhouses in Colorado Springs are typically built as either 4-unit or 6-unit groups. The end units may be built as a ranch style (single level) home. Some townhouses have attached or detached garages. You may even find some units with small, enclosed yard areas. The downside to these types of properties include the association fees, proximity to adjacent homes, noise, and association restriction issues. Some financing restrictions could be in place depending on whether or not the project was approved by FHA (Federal Housing Associate) and VA (Veterans Association).

Other financing issues include the computation of non-owner (investor) ownership. Many lenders require that there be a specific number of owner-occupied units in the complex. Check with one of my preferred lenders for additional details. For an example of home owner association maps for townhouse complexes check out coloradosprings.gov/sites/default/files/planning/hoa_2015map1.pdf

CONDOMINIUM

What is the difference between a townhouse and a condo? Briefly, a townhouse you own the land, a condo you do not. Here is a great comparison between the two: www.diffen.com/difference/Condo_vs_Townhouse This comparison will help you decide which is best for your needs.

PATIO HOME

A patio home typically has a shared wall or walls with other homes and has common areas that are maintained by an association. Most patio homes have a deck or patio and are typically ranch style homes in our area. They usually have an attached garage and are larger than a condo or townhouse. If you are looking for the feeling of a normal home but don't want to do any yard maintenance, this may be a great option for you. Here is a detailed look at what defines a patio home: https://en.wikipedia.org/wiki/Patio_home

COURTYARD HOMES AND NEST HOMES

We have many examples of these types of subdivisions in our area. The most common thread among courtyard homes is that they don't usually have large yards, if any, and they have associations to take care of the front yards and common areas. Cost is usually less than buying regular construction homes because there is less land that is owned, and the builder has less cost in development. The caution is that the association fees may be high, and this will affect the cost of home ownership. Here is a description of a courtyard home: en.wikipedia.org/wiki/Courtyard_house

In Colorado Springs we tend to see short, small cul-de-sacs with four to six houses located on the street. Short driveways and a very small area for curbside parking is available.

SINGLE FAMILY HOME ON SMALL LOT IN A DEVELOPMENT

Re-sale homes on small lots are most often tract homes in a planned development. These types of properties are located all over the Colorado Springs area and vary in price based on location, size, and finish. Boldly speaking, the further north you go, the higher the price. This has a lot to do with mountain views, treed areas (such as Black Forest), and even being closer to the Denver area. The west side (closer to the mountains with treed lots) also has higher prices and ranges of styles for you to choose from.

Colorado Springs has had these types of diverse developments since the early 1900's—there being so many different areas that to discuss them here would be difficult. Each area in the Springs has its unique benefits and challenges, and they will need to be discussed when we narrow down where you want to live and how much you want to spend.

There are many neighborhoods that have a homeowner's association and a fee that is paid either monthly or yearly for the operation of the HOA. HOAs typically serve the purpose of making sure that the community common areas are maintained, that any facilities are maintained, and that property changes and upgrades are approved by owners to keep a consistent quality. Depending on the area, they have other functions as well. Here is a typical HOA website as an example: www.pcva.org

Some areas feature common-use facilities such as clubhouses with pools, event spaces, and workout areas. I'll be including some of these desirable subdivisions in my new construction section, so look and see if the area you are considering is included in that section.

School districts are a major concern for families and for re-sale value. Take a look here at how the schools are rated in Colorado Springs: www.greatschools.org/colorado/colorado-springs

SINGLE FAMILY ON LARGE ACREAGE

There are many locations around Colorado Springs that have somewhat large lots. Acreage is primarily found in the eastern part of the county as well as some areas in the mountains. We have homes available in the forest as well as in a sub-desert like area. With larger properties, you typically have a well and septic system. Please see the section that deals with those issues in another area of the book.

When considering these properties, there are many items that are of great importance. Water flow and rights, tree diseases, land-use restrictions, accessibility, and other issues need to be evaluated up-front so that no surprises happen in the future.

MANUFACTURED HOME ON ACREAGE

One of the most affordable ways to have a small "ranch" is to put a manufactured home on an affordable, large lot located in an area that is priced well—usually out east.

There are many things to consider with this type of purchase. You will want to make sure that the property was "purged" and is being taxed as real estate. (We can check for this.) This will ensure that the proper permits were acquired when the home was put onto the lot, which is important to you as the buyer. You will also want to make sure that the unit has a HUD approved number if you are getting FHA financing or just want to know what standards the home was built under for quality control. These homes are usually moved onto the lot in two pieces, attached together, then put onto an approved foundation. These foundations are very specific with how the piers are built and the tie-down systems used to ensure they're safe and will last. A certified foundation engineer can inspect the foundation to make sure that it was installed properly. Here is an example of a manufactured home company: www.fleetwoodhomes.com The larger lots usually don't have sewer or water, so a septic system and well are usually installed. Please see the sections that discuss wells and septic systems in this book.

MULTI-UNIT PROPERTIES, 4 ATTACHED UNITS AND UNDER

Our current market makes it very difficult to locate a 4-unit property that is priced low enough to qualify for FHA financing. There is a specific strategy involving purchasing a 4-unit property that helps with affordability for you, the buyer. If it makes sense, buying a 4-unit property and renting out one of the units while occupying one will let you live effectively, for free. Yes, you become a landlord, but you live next to your tenants and it can make the process of taking care of the property very easy. I have known several investors who have started their portfolios this way and have realized a substantial gain. When you occupy one of the units you can use owner-occupied financing, which is a significantly more affordable option with lower payments and better terms.

Let's also look at some of the unique opportunities in the foreclosure arena. Even though these aren't types of homes, they have their unique difficulties and considerations.

HUD-OWNED HOMES

This has been slim pickings for the last couple of years since the market has been hot for sellers, and less owners have been losing their homes to foreclosure. A HUD (United States Department of Housing and Urban Development) home is one that had an FHA (Federal Housing Administration) loan originally. These properties have been foreclosed on by the lender, and HUD insured the loan, therefore HUD takes the property and puts it up for sale. These homes can be a good deal, but you have a unique offer process that you must go through that makes your offer the highest net offer to HUD. The homes are not improved upon after foreclosure, so they may be in bad condition. They are cleaned out for trash and items left by the original owner, but that's about it. Inspections can be difficult since many of the properties potentially have plumbing issues because they were left to freeze during the winter. There is a process to get the utilities turned on if HUD allows for it. Depending on the type of new loan you are receiving, the property can be in bad enough condition to not qualify for the new loan. I have an example offer and details on my website at www.brokerdarren.com/HUDproperties The HUD website with tons of additional information can be found here: www.hud.gov/topics/buying_a_home

VA (VETERANS ADMINISTRATION) OWNED HOMES

A VA (Veterans Administration) owned home is a home that a VA loan was completed on, then the property went to foreclosure and VA ended up owning the home. You can take a look at some VA-owned properties at this website: listings.vrmco.com Buying a VA-owned home is very similar to buying any home. The real difference is that you must make your offer as attractive as possible because of the stiff competition. The process is not as difficult as it is with a HUD-owned home, but they can be a touch under market, making them more competitive with other listings. I've even seen VA do some minor work on a home to bring it up to a satisfactory condition before selling. The offer is written on a standard contract with a supplement being provided back to you after your offer is accepted. A licensed Realtor® cannot interpret anything on any contract from any agency other than the standard, approved forms provided by our association (CAR: Colorado Association of Realtors®). So, it will be up to you to read through the HUD, VA, and any other REO (real estate owned) form to try to understand it to the best of your ability. You can hire an attorney to help if you so desire.

REO (REAL ESTATE OWNED) PROPERTIES

These properties are usually foreclosure homes that are owned by a bank, a hedge fund, or other similar organization. These can be sold as listed in the MLS. However, more are being listed on auction sites as well at the MLS. Since this is the trend, I will be discussing this process in more detail.

AUCTIONS

Just when you think you have heard it all, along comes the auction process. This process is accomplished through an online bidding war.

The bank or other owner hopes that the "war" will bring them a higher price. The properties can sell lower than market and can be a good deal if your offer gets accepted.

The process is really very complicated for the buyer since you do not have the ability to have any contingencies in the buying process. No loan contingency, no inspection contingency, nothing. How do I handle this with you? I do everything we can upfront before making an offer. Yes, you will spend some money, but it is the only way to know the condition of what you are buying and ensuring you get the best possible deal. Even this process doesn't show *everything* problematic since most of the properties don't even have the power on (for real!). But it'll help! Take a look at the terms of the auction process from one of the auction companies here: www.xome. com/auctions/auction-eventagreement

Make sure to read this agreement. Based on the auction company they vary a bit. Be very careful.

Most of these companies have an approved lender (or are a lender themselves) to get a loan approved. This is an odd process, and this lender does things that a traditional lender couldn't. Sometimes they don't even do an appraisal. If you work with me, I'll prepare a market evaluation so at least you will have an idea of the properties' market values and go into the process as prepared as possible.

My over 25 years of experience helps navigate these unique situations. Not one purchase is the same, but I've experienced so many different variables in real estate that I'm able to give you the best advice and help equip you through whatever is thrown our way!

SHORT SALES

Our local market has been hot for sellers, so we don't see many of these short sales on the market today. I'm sure this will change. If we take a dip in the market and a seller must move for one reason or another, they may come up short in paying off all the fees and the mortgage. At this point, a professional listing agent who knows how to negotiate a short sale steps in and works with the seller's lender to negotiate a sale which nets the lender less then what is owed.

This is not an easy task. The seller will be asked to provide the same basic information as though they were applying for a mortgage. Bank statements, income reports, W-2s, etc. will need to be provided to the bank to initiate the process.

Once an offer is received, all the paperwork is submitted to the bank and the process begins. Without going into too much detail here, I want to emphasize that the process can be long and difficult, and even sometimes make very little sense.

So why would you be interested in purchasing a home that will be a short sale? Simple—to purchase it below market value. You will have to be very patient, and as your buyer's agent, I will require that the seller uses the services of a professional short-sale handling agency. If they won't, we will move on, because it's important to ensure that the process has a good chance of closing, otherwise it's a waste of your time and money.

> I have personally handled short sales myself both with and without an agency involved, and I can tell you the process is tedious and lengthy. But having the right agent to work for YOU and hold your hand through the process will give you the BEST chances at aquiring this type of property.

Most agents don't have the time to constantly follow up with the seller's lender, so using a professional negotiation company will ensure timely follow-up and processing of the transaction.

What can go wrong? Many things can go wrong. But it's important as a buyer of a short sale to remain flexible and keep your expectations low. The sellers only real motivation in completing a short sale is to decrease the impact on their credit and to feel as though they did the right thing. This motivation decreases with frustration. I've seen many sellers just walk away after time has passed and frustration has increased. That leaves you, the buyer, with nothing. The seller typically has no money to do any repairs that are discovered through your inspection, so most properties are truly "as is." The seller's lender usually will not allow for buyers' closing costs to be paid, so be prepared to pay your own closing costs. There is always the potential after going through the entire process the lender will not approve the offer and come back with a counter that nets them more money. There is no magic formula for trying to figure out how much a bank will be willing to settle for, in *any* transaction.

If you are not in a hurry, have the resources to fix up a house after closing, and want to try to buy a home under market value—this kind of transaction will work for you. Just be prepared to be very patient and take your time to make sure that you are offering a price that works for your budget and that is in a reasonable range for the bank to accept your offer.

> I will help you determine the market value of the home and give you my best guesstimate for what the bank may accept. My experience helps a lot since I have completed many short sale transactions in the past. I've learned a lot through the years!

VIEWING HOMES

This is the most exciting part of the initial phases of purchasing a home! While it's definitely the most exciting, it also quickly become overwhelming. It sounds very easy to go through a list of homes, choose a few, and head out to go look. But using your time wisely and making the best choice must be done with the proper considerations. I have provided a more detailed list later in this book about the specifics of the process, but I want to go through the initial details in this section.

Once that we decide on the homes to view, I will either provide transportation or you can follow me to the properties.

Important Points When Viewing Homes

- Be considerate of other agents and their clients as well as the home owners with a few considerate gestures: park where you don't get blocked in or block someone else. Safety is always a consideration, so before we enter the home, I will knock and call out our presence in case the seller did not get the proper notification of our arrival. No surprise visits! If another family is touring the home, we will wait for them to finish before we start touring the home. This is just considerate of their time, allowing them space and asking for the same courteousness in return.
- Scan the neighborhood for property issues with neighbors, location near amenities, parking, and overall "vibe" of the area.
- Note property condition issues. I am not a property inspector, but my years of experience with real estate aids in noting both the obvious, and not so obvious positives and negatives about the house. We will take a bit of time looking at the outside of the house, the view, the condition of the siding, the roof (what can be seen) and anything else that might affect the transaction.

- You will be provided with a "showing notes" sheet so that you can keep track of what you did and didn't like about each house after the excursion. Please take detailed notes. It will help you later remember the house so that you can choose the one that best fit your needs.

- If you just love the home and want to make an immediate offer, I will call the listing agent on the spot to see if they have any other offers. This will help us in our offer strategy. We will go back to the office and do a market analysis to see what offer would be substantiated. We will then contact your lender to get a price specific pre-approval letter, and move on to completing the offer so that it can be presented.

- A pre-showing analysis (I provide that specifically for my clients) should help narrow down the houses that meet your criteria. Remember, just because you have only looked at a handful of houses doesn't mean you haven't seen the best one for you. If I do my job, then you won't have to look at many houses in person to locate the one that meets your needs the best.

- Once we have viewed the selections you made, we will either go back to my office and review our day together, or you will go home and review our showings for the day (whichever you prefer). If none of the properties looked good to you, then we will need to re-visit your needs and wants, and redefine what your MLS search is providing to you. Once we adjust the search, then our showing process begins again.

DEFINING WHAT IS IMPORTANT

Once you go out and look at properties, there will be details that start to emerge about what you like and don't like about the houses themselves. It's usually at this point we'll sit down and review what we have found and define what stands out as truly important to you.

For example: at first, you may think that you *must* have two living areas. But after looking at the layouts of several houses, you may discover that this is not as important as a large walk-in master bedroom closet. We can then set up new search parameters that meet the new criteria. Price considerations may dictate choices that have to be made.

I'D LIKE TO SEE IT ANYWAYS

THE SNOW STORM SHOWING

I have showed property to buyers in many different weather conditions. Typically, I attempt to show only in fair weather so that the buyer can truly see the house in good light, in its best form, and be safe while traveling.

I had been working with an investor looking for a buy-and-rent property. We were not having any luck finding the right home at the right price point for him. Looking through properties, I finally located a home that looked like it would pencil out for him. I called him and he agreed.

"So, let's go take a look".

It looked as though the snowstorm would be over the next day, so I suggested to him that we go look at it then.

"If I wait that long, it will be gone. Let's go tonight when I get off work," he stated.

I reminded him that it *was* the winter, that it got dark early, and that this house was a foreclosed property... meaning it had no utilities on. He did not care. So off we went and met at the house—in the dark, in the middle of a blizzard, in the freezing cold.

We toured the home to the light of our cell phones. There was a lot of work that needed to be done, but the flashlights on our phones was enough for him to confidentently declare "I want it".

So off I went to the office (very cautiously) to prepare an offer that night.

He still owns the house to this day, and it has a great rate of return. I guess it you think a house looks good on a cold, dark, stormy night, you'll think it's GREAT any other time. To get the competitive edge, I am looking for snowstorms now!

CHAPTER 7:
New Construction Housing Development

WELCOME TO YOUR BRAND NEW HOME! That is a dream for so many of us that would love to build a new home. I have sold many new homes and have watched my clients live the dream of building theirs.

But for some, it can be a bit of a nightmare.

We all think we know what we like in a home, but when presented with all the options, we can become overwhelmed and be faced with a decision paralysis of sorts. I hope to take out some of the mystery around building a home, and bring to light important considerations for you. This section will contain details unique to Colorado Springs and neighborhoods where builders are currently building. This will not be an all-inclusive list, but I will be providing links to my website that will have pictures of the neighborhoods and my opinions about the area for your consideration. I hope this journey will enlighten you about building a "tract house" and what is involved in the process.

USING A REALTOR® FOR NEW CONSTRUCTION TRACT HOMES

I often get the question about why using a Realtor® is important when buying a new home when you can just work with the builder's staff.

First, consider the cost. For you, there isn't any, typically. Most builders build the cost of the commission into the sales price so you as a buyer aren't paying real estate fees. Won't the house cost less if I don't use a Realtor®? No, it won't. The builder's development and the price they can charge is based on market appraisals by the lender. If they sell one house at a lower the price to not include the agent fee, but the next *identical* house for more to include an agent fee—the appraisal wouldn't be able to support the sales price since the comparable sale was lower. The builder would also alienate agents and the showings of their homes would decrease. Most homes in our area are sold by professional Realtors®. We represent the interest of our buyers, not the builders.

Second, consider the service you receive. The services a Realtor® provides a buyer during the new construction process is extensive and beneficial to you. Remember, the sales agent on the development represents the builder, *not you.* Your agent will carry a bit of weight with the builder since they can bring them multiple buyers. Most builders are aware of our relationships with our clients and respect that relationship. I personally guarantee to be there through all phases of construction including the offer, the initial build meeting, the frame walk, the completed walk, the final walk-through, and the closing.

Last, consider the incentives. I actually offer a unique reward program when you use me as your agent on your new construction.

Call and ask me about this program today. You will like it, that I know for sure!

> How do you best capitalize on the benefits of using a using a Realtor® for your new home build? INCLUDE ME from the start! I can't represent you if I am not with you on your first visit. With all the services I provide, I know you will want my representation during the process of building your home. So let's take a look together at your favorite builders and areas, and let's go find your dream home.

Builder Incentives

Builders offer different types of incentives to buyers. Using the builder's lender and getting a lender credit is the biggest incentive. The builder occasionally has ownership interest in the lender, or the builder has a close relationship with the lender and has confidence in the ability of that lender to close the transaction. I *do* understand this since there are many lenders in our market that don't complete transactions well. Does this mean that you can't use your own lender? No. You can still use your own lender, but you would just lose the incentive. This incentive is usually $2,000 or more, so just weigh the benefits.

The builder may also offer a VA incentive if you are active duty or a discharged veteran. Your Realtor® should make sure to ask about all incentives and then disclose them to you in full, and advise you accordingly.

Lot Selection

The major builders in our areas all construct beautiful, well-built homes. *Where* the home is located has become the most important decision a new homeowner can make. You will select the neighborhood based on price, school districts, job locations etc. Once that we get you into that neighborhood, we need to select a builder—or we'll first drive around and look at lots to best select a builder.

Once that you locate a block of lots that look good, we then review who's building on those lots. Location, location, location. Are views important? Do you want a cul-de-sac location to cut down on traffic? Is cost your primary concern? I find that the available lots that a builder can build on becomes the most restrictive restriction that restricts you. Most always the most desirable lots have an additional premium on them, so expect to pay more for those lots.

The other lot issue has to do with what model homes the builder will offer for that lot. For example, if a house you choose is being built next door, chances are you won't be able to put the same model right next to it. So, select your lot, select your model, and put the two together to build the house you dream about.

Big Options

This is one of the biggest areas I can help you with! The contract provides many details about your new home. Some of the bigger options will need to be selected when you write the contract.

Your Realtor® should advise you as to which options will most likely give you a return on your investment, and which ones may make you happy but won't add to the resale value much. They should be there with you at your contract signing when you are making these selections. Items such as three-car garages can be lot specific and based on floorplan. As an example, a ranch home with a three-car garage takes up a bigger footprint than a two-story home, and may not fit on the lot you selected. We will have all of these important discussions during the lot selection process.

Your Realtor® probably won't be too involved as you review options and make decisions within the design center—like flooring type, paint color, countertops, etc. These are personal preferences more than value issues. But of course, as your Realtor®, you can *always* call *me* to ask for my opinion if the choice would affect the market value for re-sale down the road.

The design center interior design consultants are great at their job and will help you select colors that will blend well together. You don't have endless choices and you will discover palettes that the builder will approve. The builder doesn't want to get stuck with a house they can't sell in case the deal falls apart, so they do retain a certain amount of control. If you want a completely custom home, then you may want to consider that as an option.

Change Orders

This is where buyers can get themselves into trouble. Before this process begins, you will want to make a list of what you truly want in a new home. Your Realtor® should talk with several builders so that you have a good idea of all of the options available to you, and you can keep a running list of what you like and don't like.

Once the process begins, the builder will charge you to change anything. Sometimes it can be very expensive if it requires changes in structure (like adding a window) or if you change something later during the construction process. Try to make your choices stick the first time. Builders don't let you out of the contract easily and your earnest money will be at risk if you back out.

New Construction Home Inspection

The house is nearly done, and the only inspections that have been accomplished so far are those by the overworked building department inspectors.

Should you have a home inspection completed by your own home inspector? I don't believe there is a correct answer to this question, and it comes down to how much you trust the home builder to get the proper job done. I have had a home inspection performed on a brand-new house and discovered that insulation in the attic was placed over the patio instead of the master bedroom. An easy mistake if you don't pay attention. That one mistake could have cost the buyer additional money to pay for the heat to try to warm up the bedroom in the winter. Their master bedroom would always have been the coldest or hottest room in the house. The buyer might have just thought it was the way it was and never would have known if it wasn't for the home inspection.

So, I do believe that it may be a good investment to have a home inspection and make sure that things weren't overlooked based on your comfort level.

I've also had buyers pay for a home inspection *after* they moved in. The items that were discovered were put on the warranty list and were all fixed. It just made the situation relaxed and easy for both the inspector and the buyer.

You have to also consider that being under the watchful eye of the superintendent can be stressful for the inspector to complete a good job and honestly report an inspection. These are just several factors to think through, and in the end it's the buyer's choice of what makes them feel comfortable.

Extended Warranty for New Construction

This can be important. A typical policy extends the one-year builder warranty to five years. Costs vary but are typically around $700. For that long of a warranty, it may be a good choice considering the costs to have a licensed contractor perform work on your home.

Following the Market Value of Your New Home

As additional filings are built and builders increase their prices, it can be beneficial to watch the value of your home.

I will run a free predictive market analysis for your home every year at no charge to you. This not only keeps you aware of your value but can be very beneficial if you want to get to the 80% loan to value mark on your mortgage so that you can submit to your lender to cancel your mortgage insurance. Just a value-added service I provide to my clients for no charge.

"WE'LL THROW IN A NEW TV!"

NEW CONSTRUCTION INCENTIVES

Moving to a new area is always an adventure, especially for a real estate agent. There is so much to learn about values, area statistics, etc.

Well, I came to Colorado Springs in the middle of a highly active market. There was a ton of new construction going on, so I began my adventure by visiting tract model homes in many areas, familiarizing myself with everything the market had to offer.

Much to my surprise, I discovered that the builders were throwing in the "kitchen sink," so to speak. They offered things like a new big-screen TV, paying all the buyer's closing costs, and even a new car (a little one… but still, *it was a car*).

No idea how the appraisers boosted values to cover all those big giveaways—because of course it wasn't all free, but rather built into the home price. And as the market died down, so did the free stuff.

SPECIFIC HOUSING DEVELOPMENTS IN COLORADO SPRINGS

I have visited most major housing developments in the Colorado Springs area and am going to provide my personal assessment of what the communities have to offer with links to my website for pictures and additional information. I believe it can be helpful to the buyer to get an overview of new construction areas in our community. It can be very confusing, especially if you are new to the area, to choose locations and know the amenities and prices of the new home developments.

Know that this is a moving target and that new developments are on the horizon and prices are on the rise. But, a snapshot in time can give the buyer an overview of what is going on. My personal opinions are just that—my takeaway about the area. This list is not all inclusive and my website will have more up-to-the-minute information.

Location Overview

I will make a bold observation: the further north you go in the Colorado Springs area, the more expensive the housing and the higher the demand. The Fountain, Colorado area has limited housing but is more affordable. It is a location very close to military bases. The north area not only caters to locally employed buyers, but also caters to buyers who work in south Denver. The west area features more custom homes, beautiful treed lots close to trails and open spaces, but can be expensive. Each area has its pros and cons and I will attempt to discuss those in my overviews.

Several of these developments are master-planned communities. This means that there is a plan in place for the layout of the community, any common areas, how the streets are laid out, clubhouses, the minimum size of any available housing, how the houses are laid out (what can be next to what) and other plans for the community. Minimum standards insure a specific "feel" to the community and let the potential buyer know that standards are in place for the area.

Forest Lakes

Located just five minutes west of I-25 off Baptist road, this beautiful area features two lakes, parks, and a "base of the mountains" feel. This development is currently a *Classic Homes* development. They are currently the only builder there (changes are coming). This is a master-planned community. The homes that have mountain views, views of open space, or back up to the lakes carry a hefty premium price on them.

The development has a typical Colorado Springs, tightly-packed feeling with open space close by. Even though it is located north, it is an easy commute on I-25, heading either north or south. The area is a bit higher in elevation and does get a little more snow than the Springs, so there could be days with a later start to work or other activities. This development is very close to shopping and some great hiking trails. For pictures and additional information go to www. brokerdarren.com/forestlake

Sanctuary Point

Approximately 20 miles north of Colorado Springs, and just north of beautiful Fox Run Park, is a lovely, treed subdivision with three local builders. The area is located on rolling hills with pine trees. A lovely entrance greets you as you enter this "retreat" feeling area.

Vantage Homes, Classic Homes, and *Saddletree Homes* are builders currently in this area from whom you can choose to build your new home. Access to the subdivision is good with a short drive to I-25. The area can be subject to more snow than the Colorado Springs city area since the elevation is higher. Since the area features pine trees, make sure to check out chapter five where I go into detail about land and making sure the trees are inspected prior to selecting your lot.

There is an association with current fees being only $35 per month. Parks and trails surround the area with Fox Run Park directly to the south. Visit my website at www.brokerdarren.com/sanctuarypointe for pictures and additional information.

Flying Horse

This master-planned community is just north of Colorado Springs. The area is well thought out and features an 18-hole golf course and a lovely clubhouse (membership for an additional monthly fee). Great views and easy transportation routes. Check out my website at www.brokerdarren.com/flyinghorse for additional information and pictures.

The Farm

Located off Voyager close to town is The Farm. This area is located on a hillside and most lots that are on the west side of the streets have views. There is a community gathering place (completed soon) that includes a pool and exercise equipment. The downside to this development is the very small lots and possible traffic noise from I-25 since it is located relatively near the interstate. The area is close to shopping and schools. For additional information visit my website at www.brokerdarren.com/thefarm

Cordera and North Fork

Located to the north off Powers and Old Ranch Road, there is new construction in the areas of Cordera and North Fork. The areas run into each other, so I have put them together in this section. Very nice homes by local area builders are featured in these communities. Association fees are typical with the requirements that the association imposes on owners. There are many benefits to these areas and some lots have excellent views. www.brokerdarren.com/cordera is a great place to learn more and see pictures of this area.

Gold Hill Mesa

This community is located off Highway 24 on the south west side of Colorado Springs. Colorful street scenes, a community center, and a fitness center are featured in this community. The lots are very small, and townhouses make up the majority of the homes. There is an active association for the area. Visit www.brokerdarren.com/goldhillmesa for pictures and additional information.

Wolf Ranch

Located just off the north Powers corridor is a fast-growing area known as Wolf Ranch. This area is very close to major transportation routes and has many types of properties to choose from. This master-planned community has a small reservoir, walking trails, parks, and is expanding to the north and east. Please visit www.brokerdarren.com/wolfranch for pictures and more information.

Banning Lewis Ranch

Banning Lewis Ranch is to the east of town, off Woodmen Valley and Marksheffel Road. It is a development that is rapidly expanding and has many options to choose from. Parks with pickleball and basketball courts are featured here. There is an association and it varies per the area within Banning Lewis Ranch. This area also features a highly rated school. The area is flat, and the only views are looking toward the front range from a distance. I have some photos and additional information at www.brokerdarren.com/banninglewisranch

Sterling Ranch

This area is to the north of Banning Lewis Ranch and is located along Vollmer Road. This is a newer area being developed now with some homes by local builders. This area will take a while to be fully developed, so it should be available for quite some time. The area is flat and affords little views. The area is in award-winning Academy School District 20, and shopping and general amenities are within a few miles drive. Visit www.brokerdarren.com/sterlingranch for pictures and additional details.

Shiloh Mesa

This is an Aspen View Homes community and is located behind the east campus of Woodmen Valley Chapel to the north of Woodmen Road. This area is set apart and is in a flat, non-hilly setting. Take a look at some pictures at www.brokerdarren.com/shilohmesa

Meridian Ranch

Even further to the east, off Woodmen Road and to the north on Meridian Road, there is a newer area that features many of our area builders. The cost to build is less because the commute to town keeps demand lower, and the lots cost less money per acre for the builders to purchase and develop. Winds are higher out east and there are fewer trees. Views are minimal. New subdivisions are opening as this area develops. For pictures of the area go to www.brokerdarren.com/meridianranch

Lorson Ranch

Located to the south off the Powers corridor and Fontaine, is an area called Lorson Ranch. This area is great for a close commute to Fort Carson and features homes that are less in price than their northern counterparts. If desiring to be closer to downtown or any southern location, this area may be best for you. Some views are offered of the southern end of the Front Range. Stop by www.brokerdarren.com/lorsonranch for pictures and information.

The Glen

This area is also located in the south area of Colorado Springs, featuring local builders and some excellent pricing. Located off the Powers corridor, this location is great for anyone wanting to be located near downtown or Fort Carson. Follow this link for additional information at www.brokerdarren.com/theglen

Ventana

This development is a Challenger Homes development and the release of additional lots is unknown due to the restrictions that the city of Fountain has for new construction. The development has a nice community center with pool and is located more to the southwest in Fountain, Colorado. Check my website for updated information and availability at www.brokerdarren.com/ventana

This is not a full list of all the developments in the Colorado Springs area. The best place to check for updated information is on my website: brokerdarren.com. I will be expanding this section of my website as time goes along, and you should be able to find out what you need to know. Then call me as soon as you have an idea where you may want to live, and I'd be happy to take you out on a tour.

> If you have a property to sell first, ask me about my sell-and-buy program. This program can help you save a lot of money.

CHAPTER 8:
Custom New Construction

BUILDING YOUR CUSTOM DREAM HOME

Working with a custom builder is a great option if you truly want your dream home and plan on staying in it for years to come. There are many steps involved in the building process. Making sure you are comfortable with the builder and how they do business is critical.

The advantage, obviously, to building a fully customized home is that you can get exactly what you are dreaming of. There are so many cautions, though, that working with an experienced Realtor® to represent you and be on your side during the process can make the difference between a dream and a nightmare come true. Remember that if you go to a builder directly you won't have anyone on your side, representing *you* in the deal, during the complex process of designing your new home and deciding what features you should include.

Here are a couple of points to consider when using ***my services*** (I cannot gurantee these are the same with other Realtors®) to aid you in your custom home build.

NEGOTIATING POWER

Yes, I have some power to sway the builder in your favor. Why? The builder knows that Realtors® can refer many buyers to them in the long run by keeping a great relationship with them. Therefore the incentive of keeping a source of new business flowing gives me an advantage when working on your behalf with the builder. They'll want to do right by us both, and leave you 100% satisfied with the process as my client.

VALUE CONSIDERATIONS

You will consistently receive an evaluation about resale considerations, treating the transaction as though you are an investor. I know, I know, you will stay in your new home forever. But changes can happen, and you may need to sell this new home before you had anticipated.

Upfront, we will look at the market considerations for location, size of home, materials used, upgrades, etc. and see if any of these increase the value or have little to no re-sale value in the future. Some upgrades can decrease the value of the home. As an example, if you use specific finishes on flooring and countertops that don't appeal to the general public, it can cause you difficulties with the re-sale of the home. You will receive experienced input as to what I see the market supporting when it comes to what you decide to build.

WALK-THROUGHS

Your Realtor® will attend the contract meeting, the scheduled walk-throughs, and the final walk-through. Including me means there will be an extra set of eyes looking for mistakes and changes that don't meet the original plan. Experience counts where it comes to these walks.

LOCATING THE RIGHT LOT

As previously discussed in this book, there is much more to this phase than meets the eye. Location is everything. You want to ensure that the lot is buildable, has the right views, does not require overpriced engineered foundations, septic, and deep well systems. My experience is your best friend in locating the proper lot for your dream home.

FINANCING

Builders either use their own line-of-credit or *you* get the financing as the buyer. New construction financing is broken up into two primary types: single-close construction loans, and double-close construction loans. When I was a lender in the past, I have used both options many times and can explain the benefits of both for your consideration.

AFTER-CLOSE RESOURCES

It's important that your Realtor® is dedicated to providing you with important resources over the years, after the closing of your home. My specific services include always being available to help you make decisions about improvement values, yearly CMA's (Current Market Analysis) to keep a watch on your property value, and any potential real estate investment decisions you are interested in for your portfolio.

There are many custom home builders in the Colorado Springs area, so I can provide you with some personal recommendations and information about builders in our area.

I thought it might be interesting to interview one of the excellent custom home builders in our area to give you an inside look.

ELEVATION HOMES

Interview and Information

How long have you been building homes? How long in the Colorado Springs area?

Since 2003 with 75 homes built.

Do you have standard plans that a client can choose?

Yes, they can always pull a plan off the website, but we've found most tend to design from scratch.

Will you build totally custom?

That is actually what we do the most, with hardly any semi-custom. That's our specialty!

Do you have a line of credit for building with the buyer qualifying for the take-out loan?

My customers get their own construction loan or one-time close product.

Are you familiar with the single close construction financing?

Yes, and it works very well for us.

I noticed that you have a staff member helping with locating lots. Will you go to a site with a buyer to let them know upfront what difficulties might be encountered building on that site or one that I choose with them?

Yes, that's a part of the process I really enjoy. I can point out things about house placement, soils issues, future drainage issues, utility locations, etc.

How much (estimated) would it cost a buyer, upfront, for a compaction test, well proposal, and a feasibility proposal to see if the project is in the price range that the buyer can afford?

The two tests up front that a buyer would need to pay for are: soils testing and septic samples via a profile pit examination. Expect both tests to run about $1600. To see if they can afford a project that early on, I would need some kind of floor plan at the least.

What would you consider to be your differential advantage comparing to other builders that build the same quality and price range that you do?

My differentiators are many:

- I belong to an elite NAHB builder group, where you have go through an arduous process to even be a part of. This group is made up of builders from non-competing markets that meet twice a year to discuss finances, operations, marketing, etc. It is basically a board of directors.

- We tend to work with the same subs/trades which results in a more efficient building process as we've all worked together many times.

- Our team has over 45 years of combined construction experience and the leadership has degrees, in computer science, petroleum engineering, and an MBA

- I currently finished all coursework and have applied for the GMB (graduate master builder) designation within the NAHB. This is the top tier/level of certification that one can achieve.

- We are raising the home building bar by building durable, high performance homes for the discerning customer.

You probably have a well company and septic company that you subcontract to. Do you have a general estimate of what the charges are (I know it will be very general) for a typical system (I know it is based on the number of bedrooms etc.)? This helps a bit when I am putting together my general estimate for the buyer to see if they can qualify for the loan and want the payment.

We've found wells from Dawson to be in the range of $11K-$15K, septic from $12K (non-engineered) to $30K (engineered)

What areas do you find to be most popular for finding a lot to build on?

That varies with preferences. Gleneagle, Kings Deer, the Farm, Grandwood Ranch (new, around Higby and Roller coaster), Winsome (new, around meridian and Hodgen) are currently some of the most popular.

What is your standard warranty? (I know one-year is required.) Do you offer any special warranties or satisfaction guarantees outside of this?

5 years structural and 1 year for everything else.

What is an estimation of construction time on a pretty typical (I know there is no such thing) build with a straight-forward construction? We get asked this all the time.

My contracts say 8 months which is accurate for any home under 5,000 total square feet. We always meet our schedules.

Do you have specific lenders that you have been approved with for financing for buyers? Which ones?

Integrity First Financial, Northpointe Bank, 1st Bank, Ent, The State Bank, Compass

Are there areas in the Front Range that you charge more to build on due to the distance from the city?

I don't raise my fee percentage, but of course the costs will be higher total because my trades/suppliers will charge more.

What is the one major difficulty with the buyer that you experience when building a custom home?

Managing customer expectations

Do you allow the selling agent to be involved in the entire process with the buyer?

Yes, if they want to be, and represent their clients *well.*

TIM TOUSSAINT
ELEVATION HOMES

Website: elevationhomes.us
Facebook: elevationhomesco
Instagram: elevationhomesco

THE STEPS OF BUILDING YOUR DREAM

as presented on Elevation Homes website

STEP 1

Engage in Design Agreement

STEP 2

Create Concept Plan & General Budget

STEP 3

Create Full Blueprints and Site Plan

STEP 4

Work with Design Team on Preliminary Selections

STEP 5

Comprehensive Estimate for Project

STEP 6

Execute Build Contract

STEP 7

Pre-construction Planning & Permitting

STEP 8

Construction Begins... Dreams Become Reality

THE $5000 WINDOW

I was representing a buyer on a new construction home in the mountains with a 100-mile view. This view was going to be best enjoyed out a huge picture window that was strategically planned on the drawings of the house.

Everything was going as scheduled, and the framing was nearing completion. Then I received a call from my buyer. She wanted to meet with the builder and I to discuss something.

We stood in the front room facing the framed in area that was to be where the huge window was to go.

"You know, I think that window should be moved to the left corner of the wall, it would look much better there," she said.

The builder and I looked oddly at each other, but stated that whatever she wanted would get done. "No charge for moving it," the builder stated. As the construction continued, the window was installed and sheetrock was next on the schedule.

She called us again, and after another meeting, the builder was moving the window to the other end of the wall. This time there was a $1000 cost for the move. That was okay with her since she was sure this was what was best.

The sheet rock was completed, and texturing was about to begin when the phone rang yet again. Yes, it was her again with the *final* decision to move the window *back* to where it started. This move cost $5,000. The husband asked me politely to not take her calls anymore.

CHAPTER 9:
Unique Properties and Inclusion Considerations

LET'S INVESTIGATE SOME OF THE DETAILS of items that can be included or added into your home. Whether buying new or resale, these items will make your home functionally more effective and complicated but can add some great features that you will enjoy for many years.

FIREPLACES

It is so nice to cuddle up to a cozy fireplace on a chilly evening in Colorado Springs. Hopefully this wonderful scene isn't followed up by a house full of smoke, or worse—a raging house fire. Unfortunately, that happens more often than it ever should. So, what can you do when looking into buying a house with a fireplace? What if the house has two or more fireplaces? Let's take a moment to investigate the different types of fireplaces and the issues that need to be investigated during the inspection period.

A regular fireplace is wood-burning and is made of masonry. There is a firebox, hearth, and chimney with a chimney liner. This type of fireplace requires a sturdy foundation under it since it is built of heaving material. There are several potential issues that come up when inspecting a fireplace. These are:

1. The fireplace smokes

2. It is not designed for wood burning

3. Shared chimney

4. Unlined chimney

Cold hearth syndrome is when a fireplace smokes when the wood is first lit and then when it is cooling down. When the fireplace is hot, it drafts upward with the hot air and doesn't smoke. Evidence of this problem is smoke stains and soot on the bricks around the fireplace.

The overall design could be in question. Opening a window or turning on a vent fan in a bathroom may cure this problem. Chimney height can be a problem also, fixed with a chimney extension, since the chimney should be two feet higher than anything ten feet around it. The fireplace opening size can be too small not allowing enough air to draft up the chimney when it is cold, needing a glass door to correct the issue. There are also many old fireplaces that were designed for coal. The only solution for this is to change it over to gas since wood-burning was not what the whole installation was designed for.

Long story short—if you are looking at fireplaces in a house (especially older houses), make sure to have the fireplace inspected by a professional.

The chimney flue needs to be separate for each fireplace in the house. There can be a common brick chimney if each fireplace that is used has its own separate flue.

Unlined chimneys can be very difficult to keep clean and service. Soot can be built up in the crevices of the bricks and joining material which can cause a chimney fire easily. The solution is to run a flue up through the center of the chimney. Again, seek the advice of a professional fireplace company.

A very popular option in today's homes is the installation of a zero-clearance gas fireplace. They are easily maintained, heat the room well, and are very attractive. These fireplaces still need to be cleaned and maintained by a service contractor, so make sure to have them certified when purchasing a resale home.

Co2 detectors are critical to make sure that the fireplace is operating safely and not putting you in danger of carbon monoxide poisoning. Make sure and have a wood burning fireplace cleaned regularly to ensure that the soot buildup is removed and that no damage has occurred.

A fireplace is a valuable addition to a home and does make the home more marketable to potential buyers. In the future remember there is an additional cost to home ownership when a usable fireplace is in the home.

SOLAR POWER SYSTEMS

In our ever-green conscious society, solar systems are becoming a more popular option than ever. There are many off-the-grid options for people who have an interest in not being dependent on public suppliers for energy. Solar systems have become a very viable option for most any homeowner to save on their electric bill and increase their property value.

I took a very detailed class recently about solar systems and their cost and effectiveness. I will go over some of the things that I learned in this class about systems, their cost, and the true value of having one installed on your home.

Solar System: Active

I know, I know, you don't like the appearance of the solar system panels on the top of your roof. But to me they look like $$$$. That means money saved and value added to the home. As a buyer it is a rarity to find a home with modern, efficient solar panels already installed. But once that you own the home, does it make sense to add them? Absolutely!

First of all, they add value to the property. So if you are looking for a home that has a system installed, you will pay more for the home, but the added value is *very* real. Appraisers should be, and most are, trained on how to add value to the house that has the system installed.

Second, it'll eventually pay for itself and start saving you money down the road. It's eco friendly, and will reduce your energy bill. It's the future!

So how does this all work? Let's take a basic look at how the system is installed and what to expect.

Installing a Solar Power System

Most of the time, a system that is owned is easier to transfer to a new buyer then one that is leased. Contacting a professional solar system company like Ecomark Solar (719-271-4974 www.ecomarksolar.com) for a consultation is the first step. They will evaluate your property for installation of the system and what needs for production of electricity you have.

The installation needs to be on a platform or roof with no obstruction to direct sunlight. The KW production of the system will be determined by that exposure and direction that the house sits, the size of the system, and cost will be determined. Typically, the payment, if not paying for it up front, is less than the electric bill the house would use without it. And remember, the cost of electricity is increasing, and the payment is fixed. The best way to use the system is to have the excess electricity credited to you for when you need it (like at night) by the electric company. These systems are very resistant to damage and last for decades. The systems have long warranties, so service is a breeze.

Solar is the way of the future with the cost of electricity expected to skyrocket. The best time to install a system is *now* so you can start realizing the benefits right away.

Ceramic Brick Heaters, Passive Solar Home Construction

Building a home that is "green" is a great way to save energy and help the environment. There are many different approaches to building green, I'll just touch on a few of them in this book. This website provides amazing information about heating systems and non-typical heating systems: extension.colostate.edu/topic-areas/family-home-consumer/heating-colorado-homes-10-636/

Ceramic brick heaters and other creative ways to save money on heating need lots of research to see if their application is cost efficient. This website discusses how these systems work and is great for understanding the operation of the system: www.advancedheat.org/technologies/thermal-storage/

Passive Solar Home Construction

This method of building a home takes advantage of the sun to heat the home in the winter and keep the sun off of critical areas that could make your home hotter in the summer. Check this website out to get a great understanding of how this system works: sustainability.williams.edu/green-building-basics/passive-solar-design

MODULAR HOME CONSTRUCTION

A modular home is constructed in a factory, away from the property, in a controlled environment and then delivered to your site and put on a permanent foundation. These homes appraise the same as 100% site-built homes. They can be customized like a stick-built home. They are permanent structures and are "real property".

The construction time is considerably less than a typical stick built, on-site, home. Taxes and insurability are the same as an on-site, stick-built home. They can be built with a variety of foundation options including a basement. They don't have a high level of depreciation like a manufactured home. You can select most any style for the construction including ranch plans, two stories, etc. There are several manufactures of modular homes and for links to their sites please visit www.brokerdarren.com/buyers

MANUFACTURED HOME CONSTRUCTION

The Colorado Springs area and the eastern area outside of Colorado Springs have many manufactured homes for sale. For our consideration, I will look at manufactured homes that are HUD (Department of Housing and Urban Development) approved homes.

A HUD approved manufactured home is built to HUD code and has a red certification label on the exterior of the home. The home is built off-site, transported to the location and installed on a foundation with an approved foundation and tie-down system. After the home is inspected, the building department issues a "purged" status showing that it is now defined as real estate. The property is taxed as real estate.

To obtain an FHA mortgage on a manufactured home, it needs to be built after June 15, 1976 and have the HUD sticker. Foundation inspections are required, in most cases, by the lender and are performed by an approved engineer. Occasionally, you can locate additional types of financing for these homes. Visit my website at www.brokerdarren.com/vendors and call one to check and see what is available. These homes typically don't appraise for the same value as a "stick-built" home and are not of the same quality. Appraisers will compare similar properties (manufactured to manufactured) when completing an appraisal. Cost considerations are usually why manufactured housing is considered by buyers. Price per square foot is usually 65% of the cost to build a "stick built" home (on average). The materials used in the home are typically chosen with weight considerations in mind since the home is transported by truck in sections to the site. Quality standards have improved through the years and most of these houses are built with 2x4 construction.

The cabinets typically are engineered products with light-weight counters. These homes are usually put on a raised, jack foundation with tiedowns at the corners. In our area, you will find many have a brick perimeter around the foundation. In the eastern regions of Colorado, where these homes are more typical, you will find them on rural lots with acreage. Since the cost to build one of these homes is so affordable, the buyer can spend more of their budget on barn and extra building needs. Many times, you will find horse properties with manufactured housing.

WHAT IS THAT?

TOURING NEW PROPERTIES IS ALWAYS AN ADVENTURE

One of the defense attorneys that worked with OJ Simpson owned a house on the very top of Bear Mountain. Al Crisalli (owner and managing broker of my company at the time) was working on the listing and asked me to join him on this mountain trip to look at the house.

The house was surrounded with security fencing, requiring a passcode to open the electric fence. This was exceedingly rare in our area since it was homey, mountain area where folks left their front doors unlocked.

We entered the home to find a lovely layout with beautiful architecture and a large, rambling floorplan. We walked around this huge bookcase to the other side, which had cabinets and the kitchen area... something was not right. The distance between the bookcases and cabinets was huge and looked like a large box.

So Al called the owner, and he confirmed our suspicions. This was the security *and* safe room, naturally all in one. And then he gave us access to it. We had no idea there were so many cameras all over the property which were routed to this room! He could keep an eye on everything.

I guess when you are a defense attorney, security is a primary concern. We were incredibly surprised to find this in our area, and it's something I'll never forget.

CHAPTER 10:
Working with Darren Bryce as Your "Buyer's Agent"

BUYER'S STRATEGIC HOME FINDER SERVICE

In today's market, it is important to find an expert home buyer's specialist to find you just the right home and make sure that you have the best chance at getting your offer accepted. It is also important that this Realtor® (and yes it does make a difference to choose the right Realtor®) has systems in place that help you find the right home at the right price. I am a *Certified Home Buying Advisor*™. This designation is issued by The National Association of Expert Advisors® and requires extensive training on finding buyers the right home at the right price. There are many factors involved in the real estate purchasing process. Why choose a Realtor® and not just an agent? Let's look at why choosing a Realtor® is the right choice.

THE BUYER'S AGENT:
WHAT THIS MEANS TO YOU

Colorado is an agency state, meaning that Realtors® represent either a buyer, seller, or no one and are just transaction brokers. In representing you, as a buyer, there are a minimum number of duties that a Realtor® has in respect to representing you. Let's look at these duties taken directly from the Colorado Real Estate contract, Exclusive Right to Buy listing agreement:

5. **BROKERAGE DUTIES.** Brokerage Firm, acting through Broker, as either a Transaction-Broker or a Buyer's Agent, must perform the following **Uniform Duties** when working with Buyer:

    5.1. Broker must exercise reasonable skill and care for Buyer, including but not limited to the following:

        5.1.1. Performing the terms of any written or oral agreement with Buyer;

        5.1.2. Presenting all offers to and from Buyer in a timely manner regardless of whether Buyer is already a party to a contract to Purchase the Property;

        5.1.3. Disclosing to Buyer adverse material facts actually known by Broker;

5.1.4. Advising Buyer regarding the transaction and advising Buyer to obtain expert advice as to material matters about which Broker knows but the specifics of which are beyond the expertise of Broker;

5.1.5. Accounting in a timely manner for all money and property received; and

5.1.6. Keeping Buyer fully informed regarding the transaction.

5.2. Broker must not disclose the following information without the informed consent of Buyer:

5.2.1. That Buyer is willing to pay more than the purchase price offered for the Property;

5.2.2. What Buyer's motivating factors are;

5.2.3. That Buyer will agree to financing terms other than those offered; or

5.2.4. Any material information about Buyer unless disclosure is required by law or failure to disclose such information would constitute fraud or dishonest dealing.

5.3. Buyer consents to Broker's disclosure of Buyer's confidential information to the supervising broker or designee for the purpose of proper supervision, provided such supervising broker or designee does not further disclose such information without consent of Buyer, or use such information to the detriment of Buyer.

5.4. Broker may show properties in which Buyer is interested to other prospective buyers without breaching any duty or obligation to Buyer. Broker is not prohibited from showing competing buyers the same property and from assisting competing buyers in attempting to purchase a particular property.

5.5. Broker is not obligated to seek other properties while Buyer is already a party to a contract to purchase property.

5.6. Broker has no duty to conduct an independent inspection of the Property for the benefit of Buyer and has no duty to independently verify the accuracy or completeness of statements made by a seller or independent inspectors. Broker has no duty to conduct an independent investigation of Buyer's financial condition or to verify the accuracy or completeness of any statement made by Buyer.

5.7. Broker must disclose to any prospective seller all adverse material facts actually known by Broker, including but not limited to adverse material facts concerning Buyer's financial ability to perform the terms of the transaction and whether Buyer intends to occupy the Property as a principal residence.

5.8. Buyer understands that Buyer is not liable for Broker's acts or omissions that have not been approved, directed or ratified by Buyer.

6.   ADDITIONAL DUTIES OF BUYER'S AGENT. If the Buyer Agency box at the top of page 1 is checked, Broker is Buyer's Agent, with the following additional duties:

6.1. Promoting the interests of Buyer with the utmost good faith, loyalty and fidelity;

    6.2. Seeking a price and terms that are acceptable to Buyer; and

    6.3. Counseling Buyer as to any material benefits or risks of a transaction that are actually known by Broker.

As you can see, we have duties that are very important to you, the buyer. The industry has changed over the last few years and this minimum duty list is relatively new. In addition to these minimum duties, I will provide to you many additional services. These services are not the same with all Realtors®. **What sets *me* apart as the buyer agent-of-choice?** Let's go through my strategy, and what I offer to my buyers.

MY STRATEGY TO FINDING YOU THE RIGHT HOME AT THE RIGHT PRICE IN THE RIGHT CONDITION WITH THE RIGHT FINANCING IN THE RIGHT NEIGHBORHOOD

That is a mouthful, RIGHT? But I need to communicate how truly important it is to choose the *right* Realtor®. Let's look at some of the professional advice I will be able to give to you to let you know the important choices you have in selecting the right home.

1. **We will look at your goals together** and I'll help to determine the best solution for finding you the right home. Timing and motivation are clear issues when considering the buying process.

2. **Financing your home is very important,** and the loan you choose makes a huge difference for your finances as well as getting your offer accepted. I have 5 years' experience running a Mortgage company, and use this experience in making sure we are looking at the proper loan for you. There are many options and many programs to consider when choosing your financing. As an example, the 203k FHA loan allows you to include costs to improve the property upfront, to make it what you need. With

the VA loan you can pay off some debts to help you feel comfortable with the house payment or to help you qualify for the loan. These are just a couple of examples of how I can help you locate the best lender and program to fit your needs.

3. **Evaluating your out-of-pocket expenses when purchasing a home.** Even with the VA $0 down loan, you still will have some expense when purchasing the home. Closing costs, inspection cost, and home warranties are all things to be considered when evaluating how much money you will need to purchase the home.

4. **We will look at your home purchase as an investment.** Even though you are looking for a wonderful place to live, I will advise you on the current market trends for the neighborhood you are considering and look at the predictive analysis of value, to estimate what your position financially will look like in the future. I want to put you in the position of building equity in your home right after you move in.

5. **There are many lifestyle considerations** when looking at a specific neighborhood. I will help you evaluate the schools, the location of hospitals and entertainment area, and the drive time to work. Location is everything.

6. **Issues that are often overlooked** are flood plain problems, encroachments, future building sites, and air traffic patterns. We will look at the impact of these issues to the location you are considering.

7. **We will make sure that you are able to evaluate the CC&Rs** (Covenants, Conditions, and Restrictions) for the area as well as evaluate the Associa-

tion restrictions for the area. This can have a huge impact on what you can do with the property once you purchase it and effects the affordability of the home since association dues can be very high.

8. **We will look at the total cost of home ownership.** The age of the appliances, the condition of the property, the improvements that will be required... all affect your bottom line. Landscape maintenance, utility costs, property taxes are all areas that need to be looked at when considering a purchase.

9. **I will look at all your purchasing options** including bank-owned homes, HUD homes, VA foreclosures and auction properties. I will let you know about the pitfalls of buying these homes as well as the advantages.

10. **I can make sure that you are up on all new construction areas** and what is available in those areas. Yes, using a Realtor® to represent you when you build a home is critical. Remember that the agent you speak with at the development represents the builder, *not you.* So call me BEFORE visiting the developments. I even have discounted programs if you have a house to sell before you build. Ask me for additional details.

Offer Strategy

Once that we locate your new home, we will need to present an offer that is attractive enough for the seller to accept it. Sounds easy, but really it's very extensive. There are so many details that need to be handled upfront to make sure your offer is as strong as possible. Let's review some of these details based on the loan type you are using:

1. **Strong lender pre-approval, in-hand, to present to the seller with the offer.** The loan program you choose will

make a difference to the seller. Yes, your loan has an impact on the seller's chances to close the deal. Let's look at this a little closer:

- FHA: the appraiser inspects the property for a minimum standard. This must be met even if the buyer writes an as is offer.

- VA: the appraiser is assigned by VA. VA also has minimum requirements on the property condition.

- Conventional: the most attractive since most are done "as is" and the seller doesn't have to do any work.

As you can see, loan types have an impact on your offer. Working with the right lender is critical to your offer getting accepted. Successful agents are very aware of lender reputations for getting transactions closed.

2. **Potential asking of seller to pay the closing costs.** Depending on how strong you want to write your offer, it may be a good idea to not ask for loan closing costs. There are options for this, and we will go over them in detail. The lender may have a no closing costs program.

3. **Comparative sales report to support our offer.** This can help the listing agent when he presents our offer to the seller. Remember, he doesn't get paid without a closing, so he wants his client to accept the offer. We'll make sure we put together an enticing offer for the seller, while ensuring you don't pay too much based on the market. I want you to have equity build as quickly as possible.

4. **Offers presented with a "peace treaty" mindset.** This means that I will be firm yet pleasant and honest. Most listing agents and owners don't like the com-

bative approach and turn away offers presented with this attitude. It usually means less cooperation and often ends in a cancelled contract when the selling agent has this attitude. It's also simply more enjoyable for all parties involved. I establish a relationship with the other agent, which greatly benefits my clients.

5. **Specific strategy for writing an offer in a multiple-offer scenario.** We can increase our earnest money, ask for less conditions, and many other items can be changed to make your offer more attractive. Just know, we have an approach to make your offer more appealing than the competition without just raising the offer price.

6. ***Predictive Analysis.*** So what is predictive analysis? For years I've been using a variety of programs to produce what Realtors® commonly call a CMA (Comparative Market Analysis). This CMA is used to determine a property's current market value by looking at previous sales in the same neighborhood, with similar square feet and beds and baths, in a similar condition. We use adjustments to take the value up or down based on what the house has in comparison to the other sold houses. This works well enough, and I say well, because houses never are truly 100% alike.

    What this process doesn't consider is the changes that are occurring monthly in the market. Appreciation, depreciation, new development competition etc. constantly keeps prices changing. *Predictive Analysis* helps buyers in determining what a realistic offer should be for the home they like. In simple terms, Predictive Analysis is a program that projects property values in your area on a chart, and based on when we will be buying, predicts what the sales price should be. While this is an oversimplification of the process, it at least gives you an idea of how it works. And it works well! I export all the data out of the MLS (Multiple Listing Service) for historical sales over the last couple of years. All data, including expired and off market properties, are exported and a chart is developed that slopes in the direction of the market.

I'm excited to show you in detail how this works, but I wanted to make sure to mention it here so that you have a general idea. I've experienced tremendous results using the program, and am pleased to offer it as a valuable resource for my clients. It will help with writing the offer and determining the value of the home today.

BUYER ADVANTAGE PROGRAM

I have one commitment when working with you: **exceed your expectations while getting you the best possible price, terms, and conditions when you buy a home.**

To do this, I've created my Buyer Advantage Program to ensure that you get the most house for the least amount of money. By enrolling in the program (free to you as my client), you will receive the three advantages listed below, a variety of proprietary consumer programs and services, and instant enrollment into our Raving Fan Club.

PROGRAM ADVANTAGES

- **Love It or Leave It:** When you work with me, I will sell the home you bought through me for only .9%. During the first 18 months after your closing, if you're dissatisfied with your new home purchase for any reason at all, you simply let me know and you get my incredible home selling system at .9% commission charge from me. I will list your home until it sells at your price, for up to 6 months after the initial listing date. During this period, any commission paid will be paid to the buyer's agent who brings the buyer for your home and only .9% to me. This saves you 2.1% based on my normal listing fee.

- **Home Warranty:** I understand the importance of having the protection of a home warranty when you buy a home. When you purchase a home through me, if I am unable to get the seller to provide you with a home warranty, I will pick up the cost of providing one to you.

- **New Construction Buyer Appreciation Bonus:** I will credit $1000 to you at closing when you buy a new home with me as your agent.

ADDITIONAL INCREDIBLE PROGRAMS AND SERVICES

VIP Home Hunter Service

My *VIP Home Hunter Service* gives you priority access with real time property alerts to Off Market Listings, Coming Soon Properties, VA and FHA owned Properties, and a backstage pass to the MLS—as if *you* were an agent. You will have the ability to see ALL the homes for sale based on your own search criteria (based on our intensive interview and analysis of your wants and needs in a home) and more importantly, get to act on them before most agents even show them to other buyers. This service puts you in position to act quickly on some of the best deals in the market.

Strategic Negotiation Experience

My *Smart Home Buying Strategy* is a proven repeatable system backed by market research and used across North America and Canada to get home buyers the best price, terms and conditions on your home purchase. In most cases, I even get the seller to pay some of your closing costs when you buy your home.

Buyer Satisfaction Guarantee

A Cancellation Guarantee backs all these services. If you're not completely satisfied with the job we are doing for you, you can cancel your agreement at any time with no cost or obligation to us.

When you enroll in the Buyers Advantage Program, you become a client of mine for life. I want you to be as happy about your home years from now as you were on the day you moved in. To accomplish that I have established our Raving Fan Club, which includes:

- Giving you access to discounted rates from the vendors we work with.

- My "refer a friend" service which includes donating 5% of my gross commission on a closed referred transaction to the non-profit charity of your choice. Another way that I give back to the community in which we work and live in.

To take advantage of these great services, we need you to agree to the following*:

1. Simply allow Darren Bryce of Sellstate Alliance Realty to help you buy your home which means that you will:

   - Give me your search criteria so we can set you up on the VIP Home Hunter Service.

   - Notify me of any homes that you want to see, and I will show you them as quickly as possible.

   - Allow me to prepare, present and negotiate any offer you want on any home you'd like, and we will use our skills and experience to work to get you the best possible price, terms and conditions on the home. This includes new construction homes, for-sale-by-owner, and any home you find on your own or through us.

*Other details apply. See website for additional information or contact me today.

- Inform all other agents, builders and home sellers that you are working with me, just in case you meet them without me being present.

- Get pre-approved with one of my preferred lenders or another lender of your choice prior to viewing homes. The pre-approval letter will be provided to me prior to presenting an offer on your behalf.

2. Document your agreement by signing a standard CO state agency agreement with us.

- As part of this agreement, I am due a fee of no less than 3% of the purchase price of the home you buy, and you agree to let me negotiate my fee as part of the purchase agreement and be paid from the proceeds of sale from the seller.

- Darren Bryce collects a $300 fee towards the internal administrative processing of your transaction with our company.

CLOSING THE TRANSACTION

There are so many details involving a real estate transaction that I will only mention a few here. Be assured, I pay very close attention to all the details involving your transaction.

1. All transaction timelines set forth in the contract will be monitored by me. We don't want to miss any deadlines.

2. I will review all title documents before you review them. If I catch any issues, I will follow up on them before the deadline.

3. I will work with your lender to ensure that the loan process is going along smoothly and on time.

4. I will attend the home inspection with you and discuss the implications of the findings and how to proceed with an objection that will be reasonable for both you and the seller.

5. I will help you review any association documents and CC&Rs for the property and evaluate the implications of them to you.

6. I will coordinate all document reviews and signing of disclosures with the listing agent throughout the transaction.

7. I will review the appraisal and work with your lender if there are any issues.

8. I will schedule the walk-through and closing that works for you and the seller. I attend my closings personally to make sure you understand the documents you are signing (and to also celebrate your new purchase with you!).

9. I will review the closing settlement statement, making sure all the details are in line with the contract and meet your expectations.

10. I will make sure you understand and arrange for the transfer of utilities and what to expect after closing.

This is only a partial list of all the details I review during the transaction. There are many other details, such as your reviewing of the off-record docs, appraisal conditions, etc.

After closing, I will always be available to review the market value of your property for you and answer any questions you may have.

I look forward to being of service and being your *Personal Professional Realtor*.

WWW.FACEBOOK.COM/BROKERDARREN

719-659-4000

DARREN@BROKERDARREN.COM

"Darren was amazing! He spent so much time looking for the perfect home for us, and then fought for us when the seller's bank became challenging. Darren completely surpassed our expectations! I will recommend him to everyone!"
— Roxby

"Before we met Darren, we were pretty clueless about buying a house. Darren took the time to explain things to us. He was very helpful in the whole process and also very, very patient with us. It was much appreciated!"
— Park

"Without Darren, we wouldn't have our house. Darren was a true blessing for our family. I would tell anyone buying a home to go through Darren!"
— Gustafson

The Shift: 2021 and Beyond

Market adjustments over the years have been so numerous it would be impossible to count them. Seller's market, buyer's market, decline, increase, ups and downs. It will never end. As long as people's emotions drive their buying habits, and government policies constantly change, we will have changes in the market.

2020 had shown a softening in the market with the average days a listing stays on the market increasing and prices stabilizing. Now that we have the Coronavirus, things have changed a bit. (I cover Covid-19 considerations in the next section.)

New construction is still very strong and is dominating certain areas in the market. The strong seller's market has slowed a bit but is *still* strong and showing signs of a long-overdue adjustment towards a "normal market." A "normal market" is a market where the inventory of houses would take around 60 days to sell with a modest amount of seller concessions being paid by the seller. With inventory on a slow rise and a slightly lower demand, prices will soften.

As always, as the buying season (late spring and summer) approaches, we see multiple offers on the highest demand properties during these months. Rates have dipped a little, which also stimulates some buying patterns. Hopefully the feds will stay steady with the prime rate so that business can move forward at a steady pace.

Colorado Springs is an amazing place to live and demand here is usually very stable. The military buying pattern keeps the more affordable priced homes turning over every few years. There isn't an artificial market like back in 2007 and 2008 with liberal lending practices leading the charge for buyers to overextend themselves with bad financing options. Lending these days is very conservative.

UPDATE MARKET CONDITIONS THAT ARE AFFECTED BY COVID-19

In late March 2020, our market was still very active with houses having short market time and homes going for near asking price. This may be a residual effect from the activity that was started earlier in the year before the virus hit.

The mid-to-upper income buying level of our market may not be impacted has hard as the lower to lower-mid income levels. I reach this conclusion because many of the mid-to-upper income buyers are on salary and will not be impacted with losing their income like the lower income levels may. Of course, this varies by industry since many industries are being severely impacted by this economic (near shutdown) that we have been experiencing. There will be pent-up demand as we come out of this time, so we should see a surge in business as the virus activity is decreasing.

Will we get back on track with a strong-as-it-was economy, before the virus? I don't believe so since there are so many self-employed and hourly people that are losing everything due to this shutdown. The government will be in full swing to get the economy back on track, so we will have to see what is offered for help.

I believe annual appreciation will be affected, in the short term, by the economic decline that the response to the virus has caused.

ANNUAL APPRECIATION: COLORADO SPRINGS, CO

1980 - 2019 HOME PRICE INDEX
AVERAGE ANNUAL APPRECIATION: 4.5%

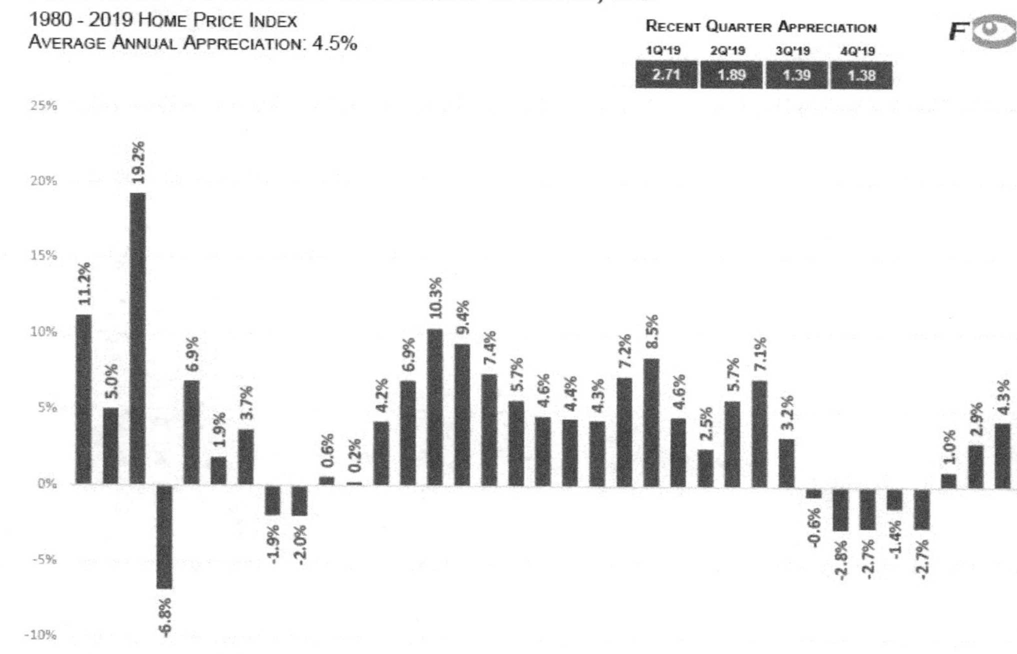

DATA REPORTED: 2/28/2020, SOURCE: WWW.FHFA.GOV

VISUAL POWER FOR REALTORS

www.focus1st.com

Lenders are currently in a mess trying to decide where to head after the government lowered the prime rate to near 0%. Refinancing surged, causing banks to respond with raising, not lowering, rates on purchase and refi loans. Hopefully this condition is very short term and the market will stabilize very soon. Available financing is what drives the housing market and has the largest affect on the buyer's ability to qualify and the price they can afford.

WHAT 2021 IS LOOKING LIKE

As of January 1, 2021, our market has a total of 419 listings in El Paso county. This amount is seriously under the demand, and market time for most properties can be under five days. Offers with escalation clauses (clauses that escalate the offer to a specific amount if there is another offer higher) are typical.

2020 had seen many forbearance agreements with lenders by borrowers requesting a waiver or deferment of payments for a specific period of time. The conditions of these agreements usually require that the buyer pay a forbearance fee as well as expenses incurred by the lender and the back payments. The unpaid amount may be added to the loan or due and payable at the end of the agreement. This will affect many homeowners equity position and could affect their ability to liquidate the property if a need arises in the near future.

Our rental market also has seen deferment agreements where the renter must pay back the amount deferred in periodic installments. Every state has its own rules regarding implementation on the stay on evections that has occurred. This has caused much hardship on landlords since they continue to have operating expenses and no income from the tenant.

2021 will hopefully see an increase in available housing, slowing the appreciation and inflations numbers a bit and allowing new homebuyers to acquire their first home without having to compete with so many other buyers.

The future is bright since we know this outbreak will be over soon, and life must—at some point—get back to normal. Stabilization in the stock market and bond market will happen, eventually, and we will be right back to selling in a hot market. One thing that never changes: Colorado Springs is one of the best places to live in the country, and will always be in high demand!